THE SAVANNAH COOK BOOK

Since 1933

THE
Savannah Cook Book

A COLLECTION OF OLD FASHIONED RECEIPTS
FROM COLONIAL KITCHENS

COLLECTED AND EDITED BY

HARRIET ROSS COLQUITT

*With an Introduction by Ogden Nash
and Decorations by Florence Olmstead*

Cherokee Publishing Company
Atlanta, Georgia

Colquitt, Harriet Ross, ed

The Savannah cook book; a collection of old fashioned receipts from Colonial kitchens; collected and edited by Harriet Ross Colquitt; with an introduction by Ogden Nash and decorations by Florence Olmstead. Cover illustration designed by Mildred Howells, daughter of William Dean Howells. Originally published in 1933. Reprint of the eighth edition, 1974.

CAUTION! All species of marine sea turtles are protected by state and federal laws, most notably the Endangered Species Act of 1973. It is illegal to harm, possess, sell, or transport sea turtles or their shells or eggs. The unauthorized destruction of their habitat is also prohibited.

Gopher tortoises are protected under state laws, including Georgia's, which outlaws the capture, killing or selling of these animals.

Manufactured in the United States of America

ISBN: 978-0-87797-387-4

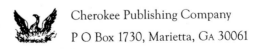 Cherokee Publishing Company
P O Box 1730, Marietta, GA 30061

TO R. *H. T.*

A discriminating taster

CONTENTS

Pilgrim's Progress is a good book, and so, I am told, is
Deuteronomy,
But neither is to be compared with this epic of gastronomy.
Some people have to die to get to heaven, and others hitch-
hike in fiery chariots,
But really intelligent people stay home alive and have heaven
served to them out of this volume of Miss Harriet's,
For as everybody knows, life on Savannah victuals
Is just one long round of Madeira and skictuals.
Certainly every schoolboy knows that famous remark made
by the late Mark Hanna:
"I care not who makes our Presidents as long as I can eat
in Savannah."
If you like dishes made out of a piece of lettuce and ground-
up peanuts and a maraschino cherry and marshmallow
whip and a banana
You will not get them in Savannah,
But if you seek something headier than nectar and tastier
than ambrosia and more palatable than manna,
Set.your teeth, I beg you, in one of these spécialités ·de Sa-
varnah.
Everybody has the right to think whose food is the most
gorgeous,
And I nominate Georgia's.

OGDEN NASH

AUTHOR'S NOTE

'Case cookin's lak religion is—
Some's 'lected, an' some ain't,
An' rules don' no mo' mek a cook
Den sermon's mek a saint.

FROM "BANDANNA BALLADS"
BY HOWARD WEEDEN.

Long after these manuscripts were collected, I hesitated to have them printed on account of the indulgent smiles of our Northern friends at our "quaint use of the word 'receipt'", instead of their more favored 'recipe'. But I found the habit of a lifetime hard to break, and my pen and typewriter were also unreconstructed, and clung to the old word despite all my good resolutions. So I finally sought the advice of no less an authority than the Oxford Dictionary of Good Usage, and this is what I found:

Recipe—see Receipt
   and under Receipt:
Receipt—Recipe—"In the sense of a formula for the making of a food or a medicine, either word is as good as the other".
So there! A Receipt Book it is!

HARRIET ROSS COLQUITT

COLONIAL KITCHENS [o]

occupies the basement of

COLONIAL DAMES HOUSE, the home of the Georgia Society of Colonial Dames of America, on Lafayette Square, in Savannah. Since it was opened in 1928, the Kitchens has won a just reputation for delightful, old-fashioned food, well cooked and excellently served. Many of the receipts in this book have been specialties of the house, and all of them are dishes peculiar to the coast country, where rice growing has been one of the chief industries.

This house was the former home of Juliette Low, founder of the Girl Scouts of America. The present headquarters of the Savannah Council occupies a building at the rear of the garden, willed to the Scouts by Mrs. Low at her death.

Many distinguished people have been entertained here in former days, notably William Makepeace Thackeray in 1856. Robert E. Lee was a guest here during his last visit to Savannah in 1870.[1]

The house was bought in 1928 by the Georgia Society of Colonial Dames and the Colonial Kitchens is operated in the basement under the auspices of the Society.

[1] Ogden Nash of *Hard Lines* and *Free Wheeling* fame, spent his boyhood days here—by way of giving it a later day illumination.

[o] Since the second edition of THE SAVANNAH COOK BOOK, THE COLONIAL KITCHENS has not operated.

FOREWORD

There has been no attempt to make this little volume a general cook book. The *Boston Cook Book,* which is revered and consulted in our Kitchens as an oracle, has made that quite unnecessary. But we have had so many requests for receipts for rice dishes, and for shrimp and crab concoctions which are peculiar to our locality, that I have concentrated on those indigenous to our soil, as it were, begging them from housekeepers, and trying to tack our elusive cooks down to some definite idea of what goes into the making of the good dishes they turn out.

But getting directions from colored cooks is rather like trying to write down the music to the spirituals which they sing—for all good old-timers (and new-timers, too, for that matter) cook "by ear", and it is hard to bring them down to earth when they begin to improvise. They are not only very bad on detail,[1] with their vague suggestions of "a little of dis and a little of dat", but they are extremely modest about their accomplishments, and they can not believe that the everyday dishes which they turn out with so simple a twist of the wrist, can be what we really admire, so they invariably add a few superfluous embellishments, by way of making them sound more imposing for the "company."

There are necessarily some local dishes which do not find their way into the general cook books, and it is with the idea of collecting such receipts—most of them having been made specialties in our Kitchens—that this little book is sent out. In it we have specialized on rice dishes, pilaus, and some variations of crab and shrimp which form a large part of our menus.

No book of receipts can boast originality, since, by the nature of things, the good dishes get copied, and the receipts swapped about until it is very hard to know when and how they originated. The majority of these, however, have been taken, verbatim, from family culinary albums—old manuscripts written in fine, lady-like hands—many of them including identical directions which have been passed about among friends.

---

[1] "How long do you cook your okra?" I asked a colored cook, to which she replied that she put it on when she did the rice, Knowing that the rice should cook about twenty minutes before steaming, I thought I would find out by this devious method, so inquired "How long do you steam your rice?" " 'Till dinner's ready," responded this wizard of the kitchen, and left me just where I was when I started.

In looking over the older receipts, one is struck by the time consumed in the making as well as by the blithe way in which old-timers toss about a dozen eggs, a pound of butter or a quart of cream. But it would not be old-fashioned Southern cooking if time were an object, or substitutes were used. As well expect to create a successful French concoction without its attendant sauce or herbs as a Southern dish without its cream or butter. But since these luxuries are cheaper now than they have been in the memory of the present generation, perhaps this is the moment to experiment with some of these proportions.

Long before it was fashionable for society women to have a career, or to do anything in the least practical, Mrs. Fred Habersham, who was famous for her table, conducted a cooking school at her home in Savannah, and here all the young society matrons gathered once a week, pencil in hand, and wrote down the words of wisdom which fell from her lips, while she illustrated by cooking as she talked. And her nieces tell me that as soon as it was cooked, teacher and pupils fell to and ate all the delicacies which she had wrought, so that the undertaking could not have been a very profitable one for the teacher. Be that as it may, many of the notes taken at that school are incorporated in this book.

Mrs. Habersham's terrapin stew was especially famous, and every receipt for that dish which has been loaned or printed since her day, has laid claim to being "Mrs. Habersham's famous terrapin stew", just as all the Lady Baltimore cakes which have come out of Charleston have been credited with being the one which Owen

Wister made famous. But the receipt given here was taught by Mrs. Habersham in that pioneer cooking school—and, certainly, it is rich enough to be genuine!

So, let's dispense with the hors d'œuvres and get right down to the terrapin stew, as they did in the old days before the hors d'œuvres and the cocktail found their way into the drawing room before dinner.

Ward McAllister, that prince of epicures, who foreswore the rolling sands of his Savannah home for the Sidewalks of New York—and became immortal over night by the turning of a phrase—ever yearned for another plate of terrapin stew "with plenty of eggs—a dish for the gods". A Savannah dinner, he declared, was something to live for, and he became so famous in this line, that his friend, the Earl of Shaftesbury, who visited him here, is quoted as saying—

"My dear boy, your Aunts, the Telfairs, could give breakfasts, but you—you can give dinners."

So let's investigate this terrapin stew about which we have been hearing so much.

SOUPS

CAUTION! All species of marine sea turtles are protected by state and federal laws, most notably the Endangered Species Act of 1973. It is illegal to harm, possess, sell, or transport sea turtles or their shells or eggs. The unauthorized destruction of their habitat is also prohibited

Gopher tortoises are protected under state laws, including Georgia's, which outlaws the capture, killing, or selling of these animals.

TONGSIN FUH OSHTA

MRS. HABERSHAM'S TERRAPIN STEW

3 LARGE TERRAPIN, BOILED AND PICKED   1 ONION
6 HARD BOILED EGGS $\frac{1}{2}$ POUND BEST BUTTER
3 HEAPING TABLESPOONS FLOUR JUICE AND RIND 1 LEMON
$\frac{1}{2}$ GRATED NUTMEG   1 PINT SWEET CREAM
1 TUMBLER GOOD WINE, OR $\frac{1}{2}$ PINT SHERRY
RED PEPPER—SALT—1 TABLESPOON WORCESTERSHIRE SAUCE

Rub yolks of eggs and butter and flour together. Put on jelly or stock to cook, and as soon as it boils, add egg mixture, also lemon and nutmeg. Then put in terrapin eggs and meat, and last of all, the cream and wine, and be careful not to let curdle or burn. Add chopped whites of eggs. Always have enough hot milk to thin out if it is too thick.

But to prepare the terrapin before making the soup is another story. In case you have to do it yourself—here is the approved method. Cut off heads, dip in boiling water for a short time, and carefully pull off outer skin from feet, and all that will come off the back. With a sharp hatchet cut open the terrapin, and take out the eggs, and put aside in cold water. Throw away entrails and gall bags, saving the livers which are very much liked. Leave all the legs on the back and put on to boil. Put into about three pints of water, with salt and onion, and let simmer and steam (not boil) about forty-five minutes. When tender take meat from back, and remove bones. Cook meat a little more if not tender enough. Cut up meat—across the grain to prevent stringing—and set stock aside to jelly. Then forget it for a few hours (if you can) and when the party is imminent, proceed as above.

MRS. HABERSHAM'S MOCK TERRAPIN STEW

Boil two fowls until tender, and cut into dice. Beat well the yolks of six eggs, and set aside. Rub two tablespoons of flour into one-half pound butter, and add one pint milk, heated to boiling point. Stir well, and add beaten yolks. Season with salt and pepper.

Put back on fire, adding the minced chicken, and one large glass of wine just before serving.

ANTOINE'S BOUILLON

A very large shin bone, one onion, pepper and salt, one bunch of turnips, one bunch of carrots, one bunch of beets, one pint of snap beans, several cabbage leaves, one stalk of celery, two green bell peppers, and any other vegetables to be had.

Boil all day and part of next day. Strain and set in cool place, then skim off all the top grease. Put in jars in ice box, when it will become hard jelly. (If it does not jelly it has not been boiled enough.) Add wine when you serve. A very large preserving kettle is needed to boil it in.

ONION SOUP

Six white onions, one pint of milk, four eggs, one cupful of sweet cream, and seasoning. Onions should be peeled, cut in very thin slices, and fried a light brown in a tablespoon of butter. Add to the fried onions one pint of sweet milk, one quart of boiling water, one salt spoon of white pepper, one teaspoon of white sugar, and a pinch of mace. Cook slowly for one hour, strain, and add four eggs beaten to a froth, the cupful of cream, and one tablespoon of cornstarch, moistened with cold water. Stir until the soup comes to a boil. Serve with croutons.

GREEN TURTLE SOUP

Buy two pounds of turtle meat in market, and boil until tender, with a bay leaf, celery, salt, pepper. Take out of stock, and set aside, saving the stock for the soup.

Make a white sauce of two tablespoons of butter, two tablespoons of flour and one cup of milk, with salt and pepper to taste. Cut up the turtle meat (there should be about two cups for this amount of sauce) and add to sauce, thinning out with one cup of turtle stock and a little cream. Just before serving add a little sherry. Serve with slices of lemon.

CRAB SOUP

To a white sauce made of two tablespoons of flour, two tablespoons of butter and one cup of milk, add a paste made of one teaspoon of dry mustard and one tablespoon of Worcestershire Sauce, and salt and pepper to taste. Thin this out with two more cups of milk, and just before serving add two cups of crab meat and a few pieces of sliced lemon.

OYSTER SOUP

1 QUART OYSTERS   1 TABLESPOON BUTTER

1 TABLESPOON FLOUR   1 QUART MILK

SALT AND PEPPER TO TASTE

Rub flour and butter together and add milk, which has been allowed to come to a boil. Heat the liquor from the oysters, and add to this mixture. Then drop in the oysters and allow them to curl on the edges, but not to boil. Season with salt and pepper and serve at once.

OYSTER BISQUE

1 QUART OYSTERS   1 QUART MILK

1 TABLESPOON CORNSTARCH OR FLOUR

1 TABLESPOON BUTTER   ½ CUP CHOPPED CELERY

1 GREEN BELL PEPPER

WORCESTERSHIRE SAUCE—SALT—PEPPER

Put oysters through meat grinder. Make a cream soup of milk, thickened with flour and seasoned with butter, pepper, salt, chopped celery and bell pepper which has been put through grinder. Add the oysters and keep thoroughly heated, but do not allow to boil, as it may curdle. Add Worcestershire Sauce just before serving.

N.B. Shrimp bisque can be made the same way, using shrimp which have been boiled, picked, and put through the meat grinder.

SHRIMP STEW

Make a thick stew as follows—Melt one heaping tablespoon of butter, remove from stove and mix gradually with two tablespoons of flour, then one cup of milk, stirring well so that there will be no lumps. Then add another cup of milk, and put on stove. Stir until the mixture is the right consistency, then add one pint of picked shrimp. Heat thoroughly and flavor with sherry.

SHRIMP NEWBURG

Is made the same way, except that a paste made of the yolks of two hard boiled eggs and one cup of cream is added to the white stew before putting in the shrimp.

THE RITUAL OF THE BIRD'S-EYE PEPPER

The ritual of the bird's-eye pepper is still observed in the old-fashioned households where the soup comes on steaming in the big tureen, and the host helps it at the table. He asks each guest if he will have one or two of the little green peppers which are picked fresh just before the meal, and he mashes it (or them, if the guest has a hardy palate) in the plate before putting in the soup, so that it permeates the dish. But woe be to the guest who fails to remove the innocent looking little green condiment, for its trail is hot enough for the "highest" taste, and a touch of the pepper itself is purgatory undiluted.

Rice is passed in the South with vegetable soups, just as grated cheese is passed in Italy with the clear soups.

In midsummer, a thick okra soup, generously supplemented with rice and corn bread,—preceded with a long mint julep,—and followed by a slice of iced water-melon, were happiness enough in the old days for any cotton factor or rice planter who strolled out in mid-afternoon for a heavy luncheon at three o'clock, and an hour's siesta after. And today, it is considered a real meal—minus the julep—and a very popular one during the okra and watermelon season.

OKRA SOUP

1 SOUP BONE	2 QUARTS OKRA
1 PINT TOMATOES	SALT TO TASTE

Put soup bone in large pot, with just enough water to cover it well. Let boil one hour, then add okra which has been cut in small pieces and one can tomatoes, and boil at least three hours, or until well blended and thick. Rice is invariably passed with this soup, and sometimes corn and butter beans.

VEGETABLE SOUP

SOUP BONE	SOUP BUNCH
3 OR 4 SMALL ONIONS	5 OR 6 SMALL POTATOES

2 PINT CANS TOMATOES (OR—YOU'VE GUESSED IT—1 QUART)
SALT AND PEPPER TO TASTE

Put bone on to boil with a little water, and add all ingredients except tomatoes, letting them boil for twenty minutes. Then add tomatoes, and cook for two hours. Strain before serving.

TOMATO SOUP

(A simple and very delicious quick soup)

1 PINT CAN TOMATOES	2 POTATOES
PEPPER AND SALT	1 TABLESPOON BUTTER

Boil the tomatoes and run through strainer. Boil the potatoes, mash, and add to tomatoes, with salt, pepper and butter.

 ### BLACK BEAN SOUP [1]

This soup is considered to rank next to Mock Turtle Soup, the beans being known as Turtle Beans.

1 PINT BEANS	3 QUARTS WATER
4 OUNCES SALT PORK	½ POUND LEAN BEEF
1 CARROT	2 ONIONS
1 TABLESPOON SALT	1 SALT SPOON CAYENNE
3 CLOVES, AND A LITTLE MACE	3 EGGS
1 LEMON	1 GLASS SHERRY

Soak beans overnight. In the morning put in water over the fire, which as it boils away must be added to preserve the original quantity (three quarts). Add salt pork, the lean beef cut in bits, the carrot and onions,

---

[1] The person who contributed this delectable receipt copied it from an old yellow leaved notebook in which her mother and grandmother had kept their favorite "prescriptions." It was the first time, she said, that she had ever realized that there was such a thing as "rank" among soups but that she would not hesitate to place it first among any company.

cut fine, and the seasoning. Cover close and boil four hours. Rub through sieve and put in tureen on three hard boiled eggs (sliced), one lemon cut in thin slices, and one glass of sherry.

BOUILLABAISSE

Although we are not particularly addicted to Bouillabaisse in this vicinity, the receipt is included here with Thackeray's ode to this noble dish, because Thackeray was once a guest in the house in which Colonial Kitchens is located, and we feel this is the place for his Song of the Soup.

BALLAD OF BOUILLABAISSE

"This bouillabaisse a noble dish is—
A sort of soup, or broth, or brew,
Or hotchpotch of all sorts of fishes,
That Greenwich never could outdo.
Green herbs, red peppers, mussels, saffern,
Soles, onions, garlic, roach and dace;
All these you eat at Terre's Tavern
In that one dish of Bouillabaisse."

The receipt is from *La Cuisiniere de la Campagne et de la Ville*—1847.

For eight or ten persons, select six pounds of fish such as whiting, flounder, carp, etc., twenty or thirty clams, four onions cut in quarters, two tomatoes cut in pieces, two dried bay leaves, two slices of lemon, a dash of dried orange peel, four cloves, a good handful of salt, six pinches of pepper, a little saffron, a good pinch of parsley, chópped fine, one-half litre of white wine.

Put all in a large saucepan, after having washed, scaled and cut into slices the fish. Add to this one-half litre [1] of fine oil and enough water to cover all. Let boil hard for twenty minutes.

Cut slices of bread, two or three for each person. Lift the fish from the pot with a skimmer and put aside on a dish. Empty all the rest on the slices of bread and serve as soup.

---

[1] Note—A litre is about 1½ pints, liquid measure.

BREADS

"TAKE TWO AND BUTTER THEM WHILE THEY'RE HOT"

When someone asked a Northern visitor, after his first stay in the South, what impressed him most, he promptly replied

"The invariable advice given by every hostess as the biscuits were passed:

'Take two, and butter them while they're hot' ".

Another Northern visitor tells this one:

Returning home after a sojourn in Dixie, someone asked him how he liked the Southern biscuits.

"Never tasted one," he replied.

"Never tasted a *BISCUIT?*" echoed the friend "Why, I've been told they have them for every meal."

"And so they do," said the weary traveler, "for breakfast, dinner and supper, but I was never allowed to eat one. Every time they were passed I would take one and butter it according to directions. And, invariably, just as I would get it to my mouth, my arm would be seized and some one would cry, 'Don't eat that. It's cold. The hot ones are just coming in.' So,

I would relinquish my morsel, take another, butter it and put it down, and before I could eat it, the hot ones would appear, and the whole thing began over again."

BISCUITS

2 CUPS FLOUR   ½ TEASPOON SALT
4 LEVEL TEASPOONS BAKING POWDER
LARD SIZE OF AN EGG   MILK
1 TEASPOON BUTTER

Sift baking powder and salt with flour, and mix in with the tips of the fingers the lard and butter. Work lightly with water and a very little milk until right consistency, and roll on board. The dough should be as soft as can be conveniently handled. Cut out with biscuit cutter, put in pan, and bake in quick oven.

BEATEN BISCUITS

Sift together one quart of flour, a pinch of baking powder and one teaspoon of salt, then rub into this one tablespoon of cold lard. Soften with enough milk and water (half and half) to make a stiff dough, and knead until perfectly smooth. Then beat with iron pestle until it blisters. The old cook books say from three to five hundred licks will do it, but a more modern biscuit machine would be less exhausting. Roll out thin, cut with small biscuit cutter, prick each one with a fork and bake in very slow oven.

OLD-FASHIONED SODA BISCUITS

2 CUPS UNSIFTED FLOUR   I TABLESPOON LARD
½ PINT SWEET MILK (OR MILK AND WATER)
½ TEASPOON SODA   ½ TEASPOON SALT
I HEAPING TEASPOON CREAM OF TARTAR

Sift cream of tartar with flour, mix with hand the lard, then stir in milk (in which soda has been dissolved), working as little as possible. Roll out one inch thick, and cut into shapes. The old-fashioned way of pricking each biscuit with a fork before cooking makes them look more like grandmother used to make, even if it doesn't affect the taste.

CREAM BISCUITS
(*For state occasions*)

2 EGGS   I PINT CREAM   ½ CAKE YEAST
FLOUR ENOUGH TO MAKE STIFF DOUGH

Beat egg, add cream and yeast, and stir in enough flour to make a stiff dough. Make into biscuits and let rise five hours. You'll feel like ascending yourself when you have sampled one of these delicacies.

HIGH BISCUITS

2 EGGS   I CAKE YEAST   MILK
I TABLESPOON BUTTER   I TABLESPOON LARD
I QUART FLOUR   ½ TEASPOON SALT

Melt the yeast in cold water. Mix the warm butter and lard with flour. Break in the eggs, unbeaten, one at a time, stir, and mix with enough milk to make a soft dough. Roll out on board, cut into biscuit shapes, and lay aside in pan to rise. In winter this will take three or four hours; in summer only two or three. Bake in a quick oven.

This dough may be made as soft as batter, and cooked in muffin rings for delicious muffins.

CHEESE BISCUITS

¼ POUND FLOUR   ¼ POUND BUTTER
¼ POUND GRATED CHEESE   SALT TO TASTE

Mix quickly with as little handling as possible. Roll thin, and bake in quick oven.

The hoe cake and the corn dodger seem to be the humble forerunners of the more sophisticated Johnny cake of a little later day, and both consisted originally of simply mixing corn meal with water and salting it to taste. The oldest receipts for hoe cake and Johnny cake (called in an old Confederate receipt book of war-time substitutes, Johnny or Journey Cake) tell you to spread the dough on a plank or flour barrel top and stand it upright in front of the fire "carefully disengaging it when done with a sharp knife." Later it progresses to the oven, and is shaped into small pones or "dodgers," each of which has a lump of butter on top to insure a golden brown crust, and, incidentally, to allow more crust per person, which of course is the meat of this particular cocoanut.

Gradually flour and eggs find their way into this originally simple mixture, until a receipt today reads something like this:

JOHNNY CAKE

5 HEAPING TABLESPOONS CORN MEAL

2 TABLESPOONS FLOUR	I TEASPOON SALT
I TABLESPOON SUGAR	½ CUP MELTED BUTTER
2 EGGS ⅔ PINT CLABBER	I TEASPOON SODA

Mix dry ingredients, add soda, eggs and butter, and bake. Corn breads in the shape of batter breads, muffins or batter cakes are popular breakfast or supper dishes, while they more usually appear at dinner in the guise of corn sticks or corn bread fritters, which make fine accompaniments for soups.

Water ground meal is a necessity for the best corn bread.

CORN DODGERS

Sift one pint of Southern corn meal, mix with enough cold water to form a stiff dough and salt to taste. Form into long, round dodgers with the hand (about four or five inches long and one inch in diameter), and place on a hot griddle which has been greased with a little lard. Put a small piece of butter on each, and bake in oven until a rich brown.

This bread does not rise.

HOE CAKE

Pour enough scalding water, or milk, on salted corn meal to make it rather moist. Let it stand one hour or longer. Put two or three teaspoons of this on hot, greased griddle, smooth it out to make cake about one-half inch thick, and let cook. When one side is done, turn it over and brown the other.

Serve very hot for breakfast.

CORN STICKS

2 CUPS MEAL	1 CUP MILK
1 EGG	1 TABLESPOON LARD
2 TEASPOONS BAKING POWDER	½ TEASPOON SALT

Beat all together and bake in tins the shape of bread sticks or ears of corn.

CORN BREAD FRITTERS

1 CUP MEAL	1 CUP FLOUR
½ TEASPOON SALT	2 TEASPOONS BAKING POWDER
1 EGG	MILK TO MAKE STIFF BATTER

Mix meal, flour, salt and baking powder, stir in egg and add milk to make stiff batter. Drop from spoon into deep, boiling fat, and fry until golden brown. Drain on brown paper before serving. Delicious with soup.

DABS

(This was found in a very old receipt book and is similar to fritters, only baked instead of fried).

1 CUP CORN MEAL	1 EGG
1 TEASPOON LARD	1 WINE GLASS OF MILK
1 TEASPOON SALT	

Scald meal with boiling water, and while hot, rub in lard. Beat egg and add to mixture, then stir in milk and salt. Drop from spoon on buttered pan and bake.

EGG BREAD
(*Virginia Style*)

| 2 CUPS SIFTED CORN MEAL | 2 EGGS |
| 1 HEAPING TEASPOON BUTTER | SALT—PINCH OF SODA |

Mix corn meal with salt and soda, and pour over it enough boiling water to make a soft batter. Beat in the eggs and butter, and bake in oven about one-half hour. Cut into squares and serve hot.

SPOON CORN BREAD

2 CUPS WATER GROUND MEAL	1 TABLESPOON LARD
1 TEASPOON BUTTER	2 TEASPOONS BAKING POWDER
1 SLACK TABLESPOON SUGAR	2 EGGS
1 TEASPOON SALT	2 CUPS MILK

Mix the lard, butter, sugar and salt with the meal, scald with about a cup of boiling water, and add milk. Then the eggs, beaten lightly, and lastly the baking powder. Turn into buttered pan or glass dish and cook slowly for forty-five minutes.

Cold rice or hominy or cream of wheat may be added.

VIRGINIA SPOON BREAD

(Small quantity for one pan)

Beat together one tablespoon of soft boiled rice, one tablespoon of butter, one light handful of corn meal, one light handful of flour, two eggs, one-half teaspoon baking powder, one pint of milk, salt to taste. Put in greased pan, and bake ten minutes.

BATTER BREAD

(Virginia Receipt)

I EGG	½ CUP COLD HOMINY
I TEASPOON SALT	½ PINT MEAL
I TABLESPOON LARD	

Beat the egg well, and mix with cold hominy, meal, salt, and enough boiling water to make the batter the consistency of milk. Put the lard in deep baking pan, and heat until it smokes. Pour into this hot lard the cold batter, and the melted lard will bubble up on the sides of the pan, and make a delicious crust on the edges of the dish. Bake in a moderate oven about forty minutes.

BUTTERMILK CORN BREAD

I PINT CORN MEAL	¾ PINT BUTTERMILK
I TEASPOON SALT	¾ TEASPOON SODA
I EGG	
I LARGE, ROUNDED SPOON SHORTENING	

Sift meal, mix with salt, egg and milk, in which soda has been dissolved. Add, hot, melted shortening and bake in greased iron skillet in hot oven.

GRIST BREAD

I CUP COLD HOMINY   I EGG

I TABLESPOON BUTTER   PINCH SALT

I PINT RAW GRIST (UNCOOKED HOMINY)

Beat yolk of egg with cooked hominy, mash in butter and salt, and put into this the grist which has been washed and drained free of water. Mix together and cook in deep buttered pan. It is grainy and very good.

OWENDEM CORN BREAD

I CUP HOT HOMINY   I CUP CORN MEAL

I TEASPOON BUTTER   SALT

2 EGGS

Mix butter in hot hominy, and stir in well-beaten eggs. Add gradually the milk and corn meal, stirring well. Batter should be the consistency of custard. If too thick, add more milk. Bake in deep buttered pans, with heat at bottom of oven.

HOMINY BREAD

2 EGGS   2 CUPS BOILED HOMINY

I CUP CORN MEAL   I TABLESPOON MELTED LARD

SWEET MILK   SALT TO TASTE

Beat eggs, and mix all ingredients into a soft batter. Bake in deep dish.

RICE CORN BREAD

1 CUP BOILED RICE	1 CUP CORN MEAL
1 TEASPOON BUTTER	1 CUP SOUR MILK
1 EGG SALT	1 TEASPOON SODA

Mash rice smooth, and add butter, then meal and milk, the well-beaten egg, and, lastly, the soda. Bake in shallow tins and cut in squares.

BUTTERMILK MUFFINS

2 EGGS	1 TABLESPOON SUGAR
1 QUART BUTTERMILK	1 QUART SIFTED FLOUR
2 TABLESPOONS CORN MEAL	
1 TEASPOON SALT	1 TEASPOON SODA

Beat eggs, then add sugar, then milk, and, finally the flour, meal, salt and soda, which have been sifted three times (this is important). Beat hard one minute, and bake in muffin rings.

RICE BREAD

1½ CUPS BOILED RICE	1½ CUPS FLOUR
1 EGG	1 TEASPOON BAKING POWDER
1 TABLESPOON LARD	1½ CUPS MILK

Mix all ingredients, bake in buttered biscuit tin, and cut in squares.

A delightful breakfast dish.

SALLY LUNN

2 EGGS, BEATEN LIGHT   ⅓ CUP SUGAR

1 CUP MILK   2 CUPS FLOUR

2 TEASPOONS SALT   2 TABLESPOONS MELTED BUTTER

3 ROUNDING TEASPOONS BAKING POWDER

Sift sugar, salt and baking powder with the flour, rub in the butter, add eggs and milk to make a stiff batter. Bake in well-greased cake pan forty-five minutes. Muffins may be made with the same batter, and cooked in muffin rings instead of large pan.

ROLLS

1 YEAST CAKE   1 CUP LUKE WARM MILK

1 QUART FLOUR   1 LARGE TABLESPOON SNOWDRIFT

1 TEASPOON SALT   ¾ CUP WARM WATER

1 HEAPING TEASPOON SUGAR

Mix yeast cake with warm milk. Put one pint flour in bowl, and add Snowdrift and salt, then milk and yeast. Mix thoroughly with warm water and sugar. Mix well, and beat hard. Put aside in warm place to rise about five hours. When well risen, add another pint of flour, knead about five minutes, and roll out. Put in pans and set aside about one and one-half hours before baking.

TWO HOUR ROLLS

3 CUPS SIFTED FLOUR   1 TEASPOON SALT

1 SLACK TABLESPOON SUGAR   1 YEAST CAKE

2 GOOD TABLESPOONS LARD   ½ CUP MILK

½ CUP WARM WATER

Mix dry ingredients, and lard, working as if to make pie crust. Dissolve yeast in warm water, and add to milk, and make dough. Turn on flour board and knead well. Roll out, cut into shapes, put in biscuit pans, and let rise two hours. Cook twenty minutes.

RICE GRIDDLE CAKES

1½ CUPS BOILED RICE	1 PINT SOUR MILK
1 PINT FLOUR	1 EGG
1 TEASPOON SODA	½ TEASPOON SALT

Mash rice well, add milk, flour and egg, and stir in soda just before frying.

HOMINY CAKES

1 CUP COLD HOMINY	½ CUP FLOUR
1 EGG	1 TEASPOON MELTED BUTTER
½ TEASPOON BAKING POWDER	SALT TO TASTE
MILK ENOUGH TO MAKE THIN BATTER	

Mix well and fry.

CORN MEAL BATTER CAKES

2 EGGS	3 CUPS CORNMEAL
BUTTERMILK	SODA
SALT TO TASTE	

Beat eggs well, stir in corn meal, and enough buttermilk to make a stiff batter, using one teaspoon of soda to one pint of milk. Beat hard and bake, browning on both sides. Eat with Georgia Cane syrup.

"YOU CAN PICK IT UP WITH A PIN"

The test of a waffle in the old days used to be that "you could pick it up with a pin." Why anyone should want to do just that has never been explained, but somebody was always sure to mention it, when the waffles were complimented! Even when they had to be brought across the yard, from the kitchen "annex," they always arrived in this crisp condition.

RICE WAFFLES

1 CUP COOKED RICE	2 EGGS
2 CUPS FLOUR	1 TEASPOON SALT
2 HEAPING TEASPOONS BAKING POWDER	
2 TABLESPOONS MELTED BUTTER	A LITTLE MILK

Beat yolks of eggs, add rice, butter, flour, baking powder and salt, and lastly, the well-beaten whites of eggs.

WAFFLES

1½ CUPS FLOUR   1½ CUPS MILK
  4 TABLESPOONS GOLDEN WEST OIL (OR WESSON OIL)
1 TEASPOON SUGAR   1 TEASPOON SALT
2 EGGS   3 TEASPOONS BAKING POWDER

Sift together the flour, salt and sugar, then add milk, then oil, then the eggs, well-beaten, and, lastly, the baking powder.

Do not put too much in iron, as it spreads a great deal.

MORE WAFFLES

2 EGGS   1 CUP WESSON OIL
½ CUP MILK   1 CUP WATER
2 CUPS FLOUR   4 SCANT TEASPOONS BAKING POWDER
1 TEASPOON SALT   1 TEASPOON SUGAR

Beat eggs well and add oil. Then milk and water, and then flour into which baking powder, sugar and salt have been sifted.

Bake in ungreased waffle irons.

WHAT? NO BAKING POWDER?

BISCUITS TO EAT WITH TERRAPIN STEW

1 PINT FLOUR   ½ CUP BUTTER
½ SPOONFUL LARD   ½ CUP MILK OR WATER
½ TABLESPOON SUGAR   PINCH SALT

Dissolve sugar in milk. Sift flour and salt, and rub butter and lard into flour and mix with hands very quickly on kneading board. Roll out very thin, almost like paper, and cut with sharp knife. Bake in moderate oven.

POPOVERS

(Still no baking powder)

2 CUPS MILK	**1 CUP FLOUR**
2 SLIGHTLY BEATEN EGGS	**SALT**

Mix into batter, put in muffin pans in *cold* oven, and increase heat gradually. Bake about forty-five minutes.

"This seems incorrect," naïvely asserts the old receipt, "but it is delicious."

SEA FOOD

"CRAB BY'ER!
YEH SWIMPS!
YEH OSHTA!"

Although the fish stalls in the City market are filled
with crabs and shrimp brought in fresh daily, the
majority of Savannah housekeepers prefer to buy their
sea foods from the negro hucksters who come in from
the neighboring watering places, and peddle their wares
from door to door—carrying on their heads great baskets of shrimp and crabs and oysters, and filling the
morning air with their familiar cry:

"Crab by'er! Yeh Swimps! Yeh Oshta!"

Many efforts have been made by the City fathers to
put an end to this street peddling, and many righteous

and sanitary-minded officials have stepped in and enfolded the poor hucksters in such a maze of up-to-date methods for icing and standardizing their wares, that the poor things have not known what it was all about. But the plea of the housewife has carried the day, and the presence of the gayly dressed vendors with their buckets of oysters, their baskets of bright shrimp and crabs, and in the spring with swamp lilies, wild honeysuckle and bay flowers, still lends a picturesque touch to streets that are fast losing their charm in the march of progress.

When you plan a crab or shrimp menu for your party, however, it is always just as well to have a reserve dish or two up your sleeve, since the weather man has to be reckoned with, and crabs and shrimp and hucksters are all rather temperamental, and may be conspicuous by their absence on the great day, if the wind comes out from the wrong direction or nature has frowned in some other unforeseen fashion.

BOILED SHRIMP

Boil shrimp or prawn fifteen or twenty minutes in strong, salted water. Pick, and serve either hot or cold.

FRIED SHRIMP

Pick the raw shrimp or prawn, sprinkle lightly with salt, roll in batter made of egg and bread crumbs, and fry in deep fat.

Both boiled and fried shrimp are delicious breakfast and supper dishes, served with hot hominy and plenty of butter.

BAKED SHRIMP

(*A good entrée*)

Cut up one cup of boiled shrimp. Pour over this a sauce made of two tablespoons of butter, one of Worcestershire Sauce and a little tabasco. Put in individual dishes or shells. Sprinkle with bread crumbs and bake a light brown.

FRIED SHRIMP IN TOMATOES

Fry fresh, uncooked shrimp in hot butter. Pour over them one cup of hot tomato sauce, boil one minute, and serve.

SHRIMP STEWED WITH RED BELL PEPPERS

12 SWEET RED PEPPERS OR 1 CAN PIMENTOS
2 QUARTS SHRIMP, BOILED AND CUT UP

Put a little water in the peppers and stew in water. When soft, mash and add shrimp, a little salt, two tablespoons of butter, and cook slowly about fifteen minutes.

SHRIMP AND RICE CROQUETTES

1 CUP RICE	1 TABLESPOON BUTTER
2 EGGS	2 QUARTS SHRIMP

Cook rice and add butter while hot, then eggs, slightly beaten, and the finely minced shrimp. Season with salt and pepper, roll into shapes, dip in bread crumbs and egg, and fry in deep fat.

ANOTHER RECEIPT FOR SHRIMP CROQUETTES

(*Very old*)

2 QUARTS SHRIMP	1 TABLESPOON BUTTER
½ WINEGLASS VINEGAR	A LITTLE GRATED NUTMEG
1 TABLESPOON WORCESTERSHIRE SAUCE	

Run shrimp through grinder, mix with butter, vinegar, Worcestershire and nutmeg. Form into little cakes and fry in deep fat.

CREOLE SHRIMP

1 CAN TOMATO SOUP	½ BELL PEPPER
ONIONS, SALT, PEPPER	FEW STRIPS BACON
2 QUARTS SHRIMP OR PRAWN	

Cut bacon and fry, then add cut-up peppers, onion, tomatoes and seasoning. Lastly, the cut up shrimp. Serve with rice border.

CAS'IN FUH SWIMPS

SHRIMP CURRY

2 QUARTS SHRIMP, BOILED AND PICKED

I QUART MILK   I TABLESPOON BUTTER

SALT, PEPPER   TEASPOON CURRY POWDER

Cream together butter and flour, add boiling milk and cook five minutes. Rub curry powder smooth in a little water, add this to the sauce, and stir in the shrimp. A cup of cream added just before serving is a delicious touch.

SHRIMP

is the name for this temperamental receipt found in an old cook book. You will have to be a good cook or a good Southerner, or both, to be able to translate it, but it is as good as it is naïve.

A soup plate of shrimp (cut not chop). Dust a mere idea of nutmeg and a little black pepper, a breaking tablespoon of butter and ½ pint of cream, a good handful of bread crumbs. Put in the peppers, sprinkle over with bread crumbs and bake.

P.S. I forgot to say a wineglass of sherry.

PEPPERS STUFFED WITH SHRIMP OR CRABS

1 CUP SHRIMP MEAT (OR CRAB MEAT)

1 CUP MILK	2 TABLESPOONS BUTTER
2 TABLESPOONS FLOUR	1 TEASPOON MUSTARD

SALT, PEPPER

Make white sauce of butter, flour and milk, seasoned with salt, pepper and mustard. Stir into this the shrimp, and stuff peppers, covering the tops with bread crumbs, and a small piece of butter. Bake about fifteen minutes. It will improve the peppers to parboil them a few minutes with a pinch of soda.

SHRIMP GUMBO

2 QUARTS BOILED SHRIMP	3 ONIONS
½ CUP VINEGAR	A LITTLE SALT
6 LARGE TOMATOES	1 QUART OKRA
2 BAY LEAVES	PARSLEY—THYME

1 TABLESPOON WORCESTERSHIRE SAUCE

1 LARGE TABLESPOON BUTTER	1 RED PEPPER

SEVERAL BIRD'S-EYE PEPPERS

SALT, PEPPER, PINCH SUGAR

Boil shrimp with two onions, one cup of vinegar, and a little salt in two quarts of water. Take out when done and save water for gumbo stock. Make a roux of the other onion, the butter and the flour, previously browned, and cook smooth with the hot shrimp stock. Add the okra (previously cooked), the shrimp and the seasoning, and let simmer a short time before serving.

SHRIMP OR PRAWN PIE

2 QUARTS SHRIMP	I TEASPOON BUTTER
I PINT MILK	I QUART RICE
MACE, SALT, PEPPER	I EGG

Boil rice in salted water until grainy. While hot add the butter, milk and seasoning. Put alternate layers of rice and shrimp in a deep dish, ending up with rice on top. Pour well-beaten egg over top, and bake in moderate oven.

SHRIMP CHUTNEY

Half an onion chopped fine and broiled in plenty of butter. Add to this some raw shrimp, peeled, and let simmer a few minutes. Cream two or three tablespoons of Smith's Curry Powder with a little milk. Chop up one and one-half tablespoons of Major Gray's Chutney. Mix all well together, and pour a portion of this mixture over the shrimp and cook until shrimp are done. Put shrimp in center of dish, surround with boiled rice, and pour the rest of the mixture over the rice.

"AY OSHTA! OSHTA GOIN' BYER!"

SHRIMP PASTE

Run a quart of boiled and picked shrimp through the grinder. Then place in saucepan with salt, pepper, mace and two heaping tablespoons of butter. Heat thoroughly, and put into molds, pressing down hard with a spoon, and pouring melted butter over top. Put in refrigerator, and when cold, slice and serve. An excellent hors d'œuvre, or an addition to tomato salad.

CLAM CHOWDER

18 FRESH CLAMS, RUN THROUGH GRINDER

2 LARGE BOILED POTATOES, DICED SMALL

I PINT CREAM	½ TEASPOON THYME
I EGG	I BAY LEAF
I ONION, GROUND FINE	DASH OF RED PEPPER

2 TABLESPOONS CHOPPED PARSLEY

Cook clams five or ten minutes in own liquor, with seasoning, add potatoes and let cool. Then add yolk of egg, and cream, and if not thick enough, thicken with a little flour rubbed smooth in water.

CRABS

As crabs should be boiled alive, like lobsters, they are already cooked when bought in market, and ready to pick and prepare in any desired way. If cooked at home, they are frequently taken out of backs, the fat removed, and picked fresh from their shells at the table. Or the crab flakes are served warm (heated up with a little butter) and eaten with hominy as a breakfast or supper dish. They also make a delicious salad.

Six crabs afford about one pound of crab meat.

DEVILLED CRABS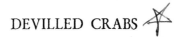

MEAT FROM 1 DOZEN CRABS

2 TABLESPOONS FLOUR	1 TABLESPOON BUTTER
2 CUPS MILK	PEPPER, SALT

1 TEASPOON DRY MUSTARD

1 TABLESPOON WORCESTERSHIRE SAUCE

Make a sauce of melted butter, flour, milk, and season with salt, pepper, mustard and Worcestershire. Scrub the crab backs (some of the negroes call them the 'bark') and stuff with mixture, sprinkling bread crumbs and a little butter on top. Bake until a light brown. Meat from one dozen crabs fills nine backs.

The same mixture, with a little more milk, or one-

half cup of cream, can be served as creamed crab, while
a double dose of milk and a dash of wine or lemon will
convert it into crab soup.

CRAB STEW

Make a roux of two large tablespoons of butter and
two scant tablespoons of flour, and when smooth, add
one pint of milk and season with salt. When this comes
to a boil, stir in one lemon, chopped fine (skin and all),
plenty of pepper and paprika, and cook well. Just before removing from fire, add the meat from one dozen
crabs. Heat well, but do not boil. Add one tablespoon
of Worcestershire Sauce, one tablespoon of wine, and
serve.

CRAB RAVIGOTE

Take white meat from one dozen crabs, and mix with
one cup of mayonnaise, one teaspoon of onion juice,
two tablespoons of capers, and a small bottle of stuffed
olives, chopped fine. Make the mixture quite soft, and
fill the crab backs, which have been carefully washed.
Sprinkle a little grated yellow of hard boiled egg on top
and place anchovy on each crab.

CRAB CROQUETTES

MEAT FROM 1 DOZEN CRABS

1 TABLESPOON FLOUR   1 CUP MILK

1 TABLESPOON BUTTER

YOLKS 2 HARD BOILED EGGS

LITTLE ONION, PEPPER, SALT

Scald milk with onion, add pepper and salt and the mashed egg yolks. Thicken with butter and flour rubbed together, and cook until it makes a thick sauce. Add crabs to this mixture, and let cool. Then mold into shape, roll in egg and bread crumbs and fry in deep fat.

CRAB SOUFFLÉ

1 POUND CRAB MEAT (ABOUT 6 CRABS)

¼ POUND BUTTER	1 TABLESPOON FLOUR
½ TEASPOON SALT	2 EGGS
1 CUP MILK	CAYENNE—NUTMEG

2 TABLESPOONS SHERRY

Make cream sauce of butter, flour and milk. Season and thicken by adding the slightly beaten egg yolks, and letting the mixture cook, stirring constantly, a few minutes. Put in the crab meat and wine, and mix well. Then remove, and when cool add the well-beaten whites of eggs. Put in baking dish, sprinkle with bread crumbs, and bake in a slow oven twenty minutes.

CRAB OMELETTE

8 EGGS	1 POUND CRAB MEAT
1 TABLESPOON BUTTER	½ TEASPOON MUSTARD

SALT—PEPPER

Mix the crab meat with butter, mustard, salt and pepper. Break the eggs into this mixture and beat lightly. Pour into a hot, greased frying-pan and when mixture begins to "set," put pan in oven and cook until slightly browned. Then fold over, remove to platter and serve immediately.

CRAB MOULD

2 CUPS CRAB MEAT

½ ENVELOPE GELATINE (OR 1 TABLESPOON)

¼ CUP COLD WATER

½ CUP HOT MILK   1 TEASPOON FRENCH MUSTARD

1 FINELY CHOPPED BELL PEPPER   ½ CUP CREAM

CAYENNE, SALT, PEPPER

Soak gelatine in cold water, and dissolve in hot milk. Add crab meat and seasoning and set aside to cool. When it begins to thicken, fold in the cream, which has been whipped very stiff. Put in mold. When firm, garnish with parsley and serve with mayonnaise.

BROWNED OYSTERS

1 QUART OYSTERS   3 TABLESPOONS BUTTER

1 LARGE TABLESPOON FLOUR   SALT AND PEPPER

WORCESTERSHIRE SAUCE AND LEMON

Drain the oysters, dredge in flour, and brown in two tablespoons of the butter. Strain this juice through colander. Make a brown sauce of the other tablespoon of butter and one of flour, salt and pepper, and the brown juice from the cooked oysters. Add a little Worcestershire Sauce and a dash of lemon, pour over the oysters, and serve hot.

SCALLOPED OYSTERS

Drain the juice from one quart of oysters, and season with salt and pepper. Butter the bottom of a casserole dish or individual scallop shells, put in a layer of oysters, a layer of bread crumbs, a little butter, and alternate these layers until the dish is full. Sprinkle bread crumbs on top, pour over this a little oyster liquor, and bake a light brown.

PANNED OYSTERS ON TOAST

Wash and drain one pint of oysters. Put them in hot skillet and let heat thoroughly, adding a tablespoon of butter, a tablespoon of Worcestershire Sauce, pepper and a little lemon juice. Let boil up one minute and serve on toast.

FRIED OYSTERS

Wash and drain a quart of large oysters, dip in egg and corn meal and fry in deep fat.

Cole Slaw is an excellent accompaniment for fried oysters.

CREAMED OYSTERS

1 QUART OYSTERS	1 PINT CREAM
1 TABLESPOON FLOUR	SMALL PIECE OF ONION
MACE, SALT, PEPPER	

Let cream, onion and a little mace come to boil. Mix flour with a little cold milk and stir into cream mixture. Let oysters come to boil in their own juice, drain off liquor. Remove onion from cream mixture, stir in oysters, season with salt and pepper and serve.

OYSTER PIE

Make a thick white sauce of two tablespoons of butter, two heaping tablespoons of flour and one cup of milk, and season with celery, onion and a few allspice. Put into this sauce, one pint of well-drained oysters, salt to taste, cover with a rich pie crust and bake.

PICKLED OYSTERS

1 QUART OYSTERS   ½ CUP VINEGAR
                ½ CUP OYSTER LIQUOR
            WHOLE BLACK PEPPERS AND CLOVES

Cook spices in vinegar and liquor. When hot add oysters, and cook until they curl. Keep in ice box in liquid until served.

An excellent hors d'œuvre.

OYSTER ROAST

This is one of the most fashionable of our winter sports, and every stranger must needs be entertained in this alfresco manner during the season.

Most of the country homes at the nearby watering places have great tables in the yards, and a deep trough where the oysters may be roasted over the open fire.

Each guest is furnished with a little bowl of melted butter, seasoned to taste with lemon or Worcestershire Sauce, and armed with a fork. As the oysters are roasted they are opened by the colored men—or by the guests themselves if they be so accomplished—dipped hot into the waiting sauce, and eaten *ad infinitum.* It is incredible how many you can eat, and just when you have decided to stop from sheer exhaustion, a great dish of Hopping John, accompanied by a salad and hot biscuits is passed, and you cannot resist this noble combination. The oysters, *au naturel,* you find have been but an hors d'œuvre to the grand repast, which is brought to a close with cups of steaming coffee.

STEWED TERRAPIN

A stewed terrapin, gentle reader, is by no means the same thing as a terrapin stew.

1 PINT TERRAPIN MEAT	1 TABLESPOON FLOUR
2 TABLESPOONS BUTTER	1 PINT CREAM
4 EGGS	1 TEASPOON SALT

BLACK PEPPER, NUTMEG, AND A LITTLE CAYENNE

Melt the butter in saucepan, and stir in flour. Add gradually the cream and seasoning. Stir smooth and add the terrapin meat. Put on back of range where it will keep hot, but not boil, and stir in egg yolks, well beaten. When thoroughly heated, stir in a gill of good Madeira, add a little lemon juice and serve.

SHAD RING

Boil a three pound shad (or rock fish) with onion, parsley, salt and pepper. Cool and shred with fork. Throw the water away. Cream a large spoon of butter with the yolks of four eggs, and add one-half pint of cream (not whipped) and the whites of four eggs whipped stiff. Season with salt, paprika and sherry and add fish. Butter a mold, put in the mixture, set in a pan of water and cook three-quarters of an hour. Before removing from oven, try with a knife, as you do custard. Turn out on platter, fill center with boiled shrimp, and pour a cream sauce with mushrooms over all.

For a simpler dish, a cheese sauce is a good substitute.

BAKED SHAD WITH ROE

Split and clean a three or four pound roe shad, and fill with a stuffing made with Irish potatoes, salt, pepper, and a small piece of bacon. Put shad in pan with a little water, a bay leaf, and a piece of butter, and baste constantly until done. The roe may be broiled in the pan with the fish, or broiled separately and served with it. Garnish fish with parsley and lemon.

BOILED FISH WITH SAUCE

Cut up two onions and put in pot with one tablespoon of butter and cook. Then add five pounds of bass or red fish, cut in good sized pieces, with water enough to cover, two sliced lemons, black and red pepper and a dash of nutmeg.

When fish is thoroughly done, remove and put on platter with the following sauce.

Beat six eggs, and add one-half cup of vinegar, one tablespoon of flour (rubbed smooth in a little water) and some of the hot fish sauce. Cook a few minutes until the consistency of custard, pour over fish, and serve immediately.

DRUM FISH ROE

Tie up the roe you want to cook in cheesecloth, and boil in salted water until well done and tender. Take out of cloth and put on ice. When cold, slice across in pieces about one-quarter of an inch thick, roll in egg and flour and fry.

BAKED FISH WITH SAUCE

Boil one large fish, remove the bones and cut in small pieces (also using the roe, if shad). Put on one quart of milk to boil, and thicken it with a cup of flour which has been rubbed smooth with one-half cup of butter. Season with chopped onion and parsley, nutmeg, salt, pepper, and the rind of two lemons. Stir in the yolks of two eggs and cook until thick. A glass of wine is a happy addition.

Butter a baking dish or casserole. Put in one layer of fish, a layer of sauce, and so on to the top, sprinkling the last layer with bread crumbs and butter, and baking slowly for one hour. Individual shells can be used if desired.

TURBOT À LA CRÊME

Boil a five or six pound haddock, or any large, coarse-grained fish, remove all bones, and shred fine.

Let a quart of milk, into which you have put a quarter of an onion and a piece of parsley, come to boil. Stir in a scant cup of flour which has been mixed with a cup of cold meat and two egg yolks, and season well with salt, and with one-half teaspoon of white pepper, one-half teaspoon of thyme, one-half cup of butter.

Butter a pan and put in a layer of sauce, then a layer of fish, then sauce again, sprinkle the top with bread crumbs and grated cheese, and bake a light brown.

AN OLD-FASHIONED SOUTHERN DINNER

"Some features of the everyday Southern dinner," says Ward McAllister in *Society as I Have Found It*, "were pilau (boiled chicken on a bed of rice with bacon), hopping john, okra soup, shrimp pie, Pompey head [1] (a stuffed filet of veal), roast quail and snipe during the season, and shad daily, boiled, broiled and baked."

Mr. McAllister gives the following as a typical menu:

Terrapin Soup and Oyster Soup or Mock Turtle Soup
Soft Shell or Cylindrical Nose Turtle
Boiled Fresh Water Trout (known with us at the North as Chub)
Shad stuffed and baked (We broil it)
Boiled Turkey, Oyster sauce—a roast pea-hen
Boiled Southern Ham
Escalloped Oysters—Maccaroni with Cheese—Prawn Pie
Crabs stuffed in shell
Roast Ducks—A haunch of venison
Dessert
Plum Pudding—Mince pies—Trifle—Floating Island
Blanc Mange—Jelly—Ice Cream.

---

[1] This dish came on black with cloves, which probably suggested the descriptive name.

CHICKEN, GAME, MEATS

FRIED CHICKEN

Since it seems to be the general impression that in the South we eat fried chicken for breakfast, dinner and supper, the honor place shall be given that dish in this, the meat section. There are receipts galore for this delicacy, but the good old-fashioned way when it comes to the table fairly stewing in its own juice, seems to me the best of all.

All the directions agree on the preliminary activities—to wit: Cut up the chicken, sprinkle with salt and pepper, dredge with flour, and fry in deep, and very hot, fat. But as some like it wet and some like it dry, the *modus operandi* seems to vary a little at this point. If you are going to take it on a picnic, stop just where you are in the proceedings, and pack your kit. If you are going to eat it at once, remove the chicken from the grease, and keep it warm until you have made the gravy. Pour off most of the fat in which the chicken has been fried, leaving a little in the pan. To this, add a large tablespoon of flour, and cook, stirring it constantly, until a golden brown. Season with salt and pepper, add one-half cup of cream, heat thoroughly and pour over the chicken.

It makes my mouth water to write about it!

CHICKEN FRICASSEE

1 CHICKEN, 1 EGG (AND IT DOESN'T MAKE ANY DIFFERENCE
IN THIS CASE WHICH COMES FIRST)

2 TABLESPOONS FLOUR   1 CUP MILK

2 TABLESPOONS BUTTER   SALT, PEPPER

Boil the chicken until done, and cut up for serving. Make a sauce of the butter, flour, milk, and one well-beaten egg, seasoned with salt and pepper. Add to this two hard boiled eggs, cut up, and pour over the chicken. Let stew together a few minutes and serve.

COLONIAL WARRIORS' CHICKEN PIE

This delectable dish has come to be known as "Colonial Warriors' Chicken Pie," because it is always the *pièce de résistance* of the basket luncheon at the annual river trip which the Society of Colonial Wars gives in the Spring.

Select a young hen of six or seven pounds, not too fat. Have cleaned and kept in the refrigerator twenty-four hours. Boil as you would for salad, using any seasoning you prefer (we use only salt, pepper and a little celery). Put aside in the water in which it was cooked for another twenty-four hours. This not only makes the meat tender, but as the fat rises it can be discarded if there is too much.

Cut in halves the mushrooms from two cans of French mushrooms (fresh may be used but give the pie a dark color), and slice one dozen hard boiled eggs.

Cut the chicken in dice, place a layer of this on the bottom of a deep baking dish, a layer of mushrooms, a layer of eggs, and so on until the dish is full. In the meantime, the stock in which the chicken has been cooked should have boiled down until it has been reduced one-half. Pour this over dish, cover with a very short pie crust, and bake.

RICE AND CHICKEN PIE

1 PINT RICE	1 TABLESPOON BUTTER
SCANT PINT MILK	2 EGGS
1 CUT UP CHICKEN	

Boil rice in salted water until soft. Stir in the butter while it is hot, and add the milk and eggs. Put one layer of this in baking dish, then the chicken, then a crust of rice. Bake until a light brown.

RICE AND CHICKEN PIE WITH CURRY

Cut up chicken as for frying, and stew it with giblets and a little bacon until tender. Remove bones, and season gravy with one teaspoon of curry powder, pepper, a tablespoon of butter, and onion and a little parsley. Put a layer of boiled rice in an earthen dish, then a layer of chicken. Pour gravy over this, cover with a layer of rice and bake about one hour.

CHICKEN PIE

One pair of fowls, boiled until tender. Remove bones and put bones back into liquor in which fowls were boiled, with one onion, salt, and pepper. Boil and strain. Cut up white meat. Run dark meat and skin through chopper, and add to white meat. Melt one quarter pound of butter, four tablespoons of flour, add chicken jelly slowly, then chicken meat, then one can of mushrooms, six hard boiled eggs chopped fine, salt and pepper, and let all cook together. Line a baking dish with pie crust, and bake it in oven. When a light brown, pour in mushrooms and chicken, then put crust on top and bake again.

CHICKEN TERRAPIN

Parboil and skin two sets of sweet breads and cut in dice. Boil two chickens, cut up with the above, and season. Put into a double boiler one quart of cream, thicken with an even tablespoon of cornstarch, and let it get hot. Stir in carefully the well-beaten yolks of two eggs, and a teaspoon of butter, and season with salt and red pepper. When well thickened and hot (not boiling) stir in the chicken and sweet breads, and add last of all a wineglass of sherry.

JELLIED CHICKEN

Soak two tablespoons of gelatine in a little cold
water, and dissolve in small quantity of hot water.
Stir into this one-half cup of mayonnaise, one-half cup
of whipped cream, one-third cup of minced celery,
three-fourths tablespoon of lemon juice, one and one-
half cups of minced chicken, and one-quarter cup of
stuffed olives, chopped fine. Transfer to small molds
and set aside to congeal. Turn out on thick slices of
tomato.

CHICKEN GUMBO

1 LARGE CHICKEN	2 CANS TOMATOES
½ SMALL RED PEPPER	2 CANS CORN
SPRIG PARSLEY, CHOPPED	1 TEASPOON SUGAR
1 QUART OKRA	1 PINT BUTTER BEANS
4 TABLESPOONS BUTTER	3 TABLESPOONS FLOUR
SALT TO TASTE	

Cut up the chicken as for frying, and fry in boiler
in which the gumbo is to be made. Fry until butter is
brown, then add four quarts water, and cook until meat
leaves bones. Remove latter.

Brown flour in butter, add all vegetables and cook a
few minutes, then add to stock and cook until vegetables are tender and gumbo is thick.

CHICKEN OR TURKEY STEW

2 CUPS COLD DICED CHICKEN OR TURKEY

2 HARD BOILED EGGS   1 TABLESPOON BUTTER

2 TABLESPOONS FLOUR   1 CAN MUSHROOMS

A LITTLE GRATED NUTMEG

A LITTLE LEMON JUICE AND RIND OF $\frac{1}{4}$ LEMON

1 TEASPOON WORCESTERSHIRE SAUCE

CHICKEN OR TURKEY STOCK

Rub the yolks of eggs and butter together, then add flour and chicken or turkey stock, the liquor from the mushrooms, and seasoning. Add chicken or turkey and mushrooms, and the chopped whites of eggs just before serving. The mushrooms may be omitted.

A POSSUM HUNT

A cold night in January is usually selected for this popular alfresco evening's entertainment.

The crowd collects at some country house, or convenient cross-roads, and makes into the woods with trained hounds, following them across hill and dale, through underbrush and swamps, until the dogs have treed their game, when they stand under the tree yelping like nothing human, until the crowd gathers and tries to coax Br' Possum down.

In the old days when only lanterns were available for such sport, the correct thing was to shake the possum out, but in nine times out of ten the dogs got away with the prize, so large flashlights are taken along now and turned on the tree, and the poor old possum hasn't a chance. First you see a piece of Spanish moss, which you mistake for your prize, or a bunch of mistletoe may deceive you, but suddenly two bright eyes burn from a silent mass and you know you have him in your reach, and some one climbs up and quietly takes him. A rabbit may run, but a possum will never move, and when once you catch his gleaming eye, it is all up with him, and in short order he is dropped safely into a crocus sack and headed for home.

POSSUM AND 'TATERS

While it is generally conceded that the fun lies more in the chase of the elusive coon than in the eating, there are those who hold that possum and 'taters is a most delectable diet, so here is the prescription for cooking your game after you have bagged it.

Before you go to bed that night scald the possum with lye and scrape off the hair. (Or have it done, which would be altogether more pleasant all around.) Dress whole, leaving on head and tail. Rub well with salt and put in a cool place overnight.

When ready to cook, put in a deep pan with one quart of water, place three or four slices of breakfast bacon reverently across his breast, and put in oven. When half done, remove from oven and stuff with a dressing made of bread crumbs, a little onion, salt and pepper and possum juice taken from the pan in which he has been reposing. Return him to pan, and place around him some small peeled sweet potatoes, and bake all until a light brown, basting frequently with the gravy.

A GOOD HASH

In the South, where some people are still guilty of eating a comfortable breakfast, this economical receipt is very popular.

I SMALL CUP WATER	½ TEASPOON CHOPPED ONION
½ TEASPOON LEMON JUICE	I TEASPOON CHOPPED PARSLEY
I TABLESPOON BUTTER	I TEASPOON FLOUR
I CUP OF ANY KIND OF COLD MEAT, CHOPPED FINE	

Make a sauce by stewing together the water, onion, lemon juice and parsley, thickened with the flour and butter which have been rubbed together. Just before serving, add the meat and heat well, but do not cook.

VEAL WITH CURRY POWDER

2 POUNDS ROUND VEAL	2 MEDIUM SIZED ONIONS
I TABLESPOON BUTTER	I TEASPOON CURRY POWDER
I TABLESPOON FLOUR	

Stew veal, and strew over it the onions. Rub together the butter and curry and flour, and add to this a cup of the broth in which the meat was cooked. Stew for five minutes, and when the meat is done, take up and serve with this hot curry gravy.

Chicken and turtle are excellent cooked this way.

CASEROLE OF BEEF

5 POUNDS ROUND BEEF (SHOULDER CLOD)
4 TABLESPOONS WORCESTERSHIRE SAUCE

1 TABLESPOON VINEGAR	1 TEASPOON CELERY SEED
3 SMALL WHITE ONIONS	6 CLOVES
2 SLICES BACON	PINCH MUSTARD
A LITTLE NUTMEG	½ CUP FLOUR

SALT AND PEPPER

Sear the beef on both sides to keep the juices in. Brown the flour and sprinkle over beef. Season with salt, pepper, and put in iron pot with vinegar, onions (cut up), Worcestershire Sauce, cloves, celery seed, nutmeg and mustard. Lay bacon across the top, cover two-thirds with cold water, put in oven, and cook slowly for four hours.

Potatoes placed around this and allowed to cook slowly with the meat have a delicious flavor.

SCOTCH COLLOPS

Two pounds of round of beef, put through the meat grinder. Remove all strings, and season with salt and pepper, a pinch of allspice, and a little thyme. Put a tablespoon of finely chopped white meat and a teaspoon of butter and a teaspoon of finely chopped onion in a saucepan, and cook together and then add the ground beef. Stir often, and add one-half cup of tomato juice. Stir until thoroughly done. Can have it soft or dry, as preferred.

RICE BIRDS

If you can eat with relish the beef and lark pie for which the Cheshire Cheese is famous, you will be sure to appreciate how delicate a thing is our rice bird pilau, for which the receipt is given below.

These tiny birds, known as reed birds in Philadelphia, and as bobolinks in New England, flock to the rice fields in large numbers in the late summer. In the old days they were such a pest that the planters would pay the negroes to kill them, and the markets were surfeited with the little game. Alas, now, with the passing of the rice culture in this part of the country—and of the bird laws as well—they are a rare delicacy, indeed!

TO COOK RICE BIRDS

"Select the fattest birds," says the *Carolina House-wife*, an old cook book long out of print . . . but my advice is to take any birds that come your way and be thankful. And "permit no sacrilegious hand to remove the head," continues this ancient oracle, "for at the base of the brain of the rice bird is the most succulent portion. They should be either baked whole, split and broiled, or placed in a pan with a lump of butter, pepper and salt, and cooked over a quick fire."

RICE BIRD PILAU

Stew one dozen rice birds in a quart of water, until thoroughly done, seasoning them to taste with red pepper and salt. When done, remove birds and sprinkle one pint of rice in the water in which they were cooked. Boil fifteen minutes, then drain off water, stir in the birds, and steam until the rice is dry and grainy. And when the pie is opened . . . even if the birds don't begin to sing, you will have to admit that the dish is fit to set before a King!

TO COOK DUCKS

Pick birds carefully, removing pin feathers—to skin them is a crime.

Stuff with few slices of raw apples, or onions or carrots. Place in a deep pan or casserole dish with cover. Pin two or three slices of bacon or salt pork across the breast of each duck, and place another in the bottom of the dish. Pour a wineglass of water over this, sprinkle generously with black pepper, place cover on tight, and set in hot oven. Allow birds to steam this way one-half hour. Then remove cover, and let them brown nicely on top. Cook as done as you please, but the juice will always run as you slice the breast.

VENISON

Soak a saddle of venison in cold water. Peel off the thick skin, and lard it with white meat or bacon (that is, cut slits in the venison with a sharp knife, and insert slices of bacon). Put a little water in the pan, and plenty of Worcestershire Sauce, and cook like any other roast, basting frequently.

VENISON STEAKS

Should be fried with very little lard, or butter, turning frequently. "They should be treated as a child, and never be let alone a moment," says the old cook who gave me the venison receipt. And when they are fried to a turn, they should be covered, and allowed to simmer slowly until tender. The backstrap is the best to use for steaks. Slice with the grain of the meat, pieces of about one inch thick. Broil in butter with pepper and salt to taste. Just before taking off add sherry wine to flavor.

BOILED HAM

Wash a ten pound ham carefully, and scrub with a brush. Soak in cold water overnight. Next morning, put it in a ham boiler, skin side down, cover well with cold water into which you put one cup of black molasses, one cup of vinegar, one onion and one apple. Boil until well done, and leave in water overnight. On the morning of the second day, remove the skin, cover with a thick paste made of dry mustard, one cup of brown sugar and a little Worcestershire Sauce. Stick full of cloves, put in the oven and bake.

BAKED HAM

(Fortunately this is not quite as complicated as it sounds)

Take any good ham, not necessarily a very expensive one, wash it well and put it in a large boiler, skin side up. Pour over it one can of black molasses and four quarts of weak tea!—pouring the tea in the empty syrup can to see that no sweetness lingers behind—and let it soak in this sweet bath overnight.

Next morning, put ham in steamer—fat side up this time—and pour over it about two quarts of water, and bake in covered steamer three or four hours.

Take out, skin, and plaster it with a paste made of tomato catsup and mustard. Return it to the oven in this new dress and let it cook about half an hour, basting it frequently with a bottle of beer! Then sprinkle with brown sugar, bake until a little browner, and serve while hot.

Good? Well, you'd be surprised.

The strange ingredients for this proceeding include, besides the ham: one large can black molasses, one cup of tomato catsup, several tablespoons of mustard, four

7

---

quarts of weak tea, one bottle of beer and one cup of brown sugar.

ARROZ AMARILLO

Boil a hen until tender, pull off the meat and cut in one-half-inch cubes. Rub olive oil over the inside of a casserole, put in the chicken cubes and add:

4 CUPS WELL WASHED RAW RICE	10 CARROTS
4 LARGE IRISH POTATOES, DICED	8 SHALLOTS
1 SMALL PIECE OF CHOPPED GARLIC	
1 TEASPOON CHOPPED PARSLEY	
1 TEA CUP GREEN PEAS	1 CAN MUSHROOM AND LIQUOR
1 LARGE ONION, CUT UP AND BROWNED IN OLIVE OIL	
(ADD BOTH OIL AND ONION)	
2 TEASPOONS SALT	1 CAN PIMENTO, DICED
4 SALT SPOONS SPANISH SAFFRON	
2 SALT SPOONS GROUND THYME	
2 TEASPOONS WHITE PEPPER [1]	

Stir all well together. Cover completely with the stock the hen was boiled in. Cover with an oiled piece of brown paper and put casserole top over all. Cook in a slow oven. If the mixture is too dry, before getting done, be sure to add hot stock or hot water.

[1] No, don't add the Kitchen stove. You will need that to cook it in.

RICE AND HOMINY DISHES

TO THE BIG HOUSE

In most of the South, and particularly along the coast where rice plantations once thrived, rice and hominy are served daily in various guises. Boiled hominy is an invariable breakfast and supper dish, and boiled rice is served as regularly for dinner as Irish (or white) potatoes are in the North.

The only exception to this rule is that rice is never served with fish, and there is an old story of the butler who was horrified when a guest in the house asked for rice with his fish. . . . "Suh," replied this butler, whom half the old families claim as their own,[1] "in dis house we don't eat rice wid our fish."

---

[1] Ward McAllister tells this story in his book, and says it was *their* butler!

Be that as it may, boiled hominy and butter for breakfast as an accompaniment to shrimp, or sausages or bacon, according to the season, and a plate piled high with white fluffy rice for dinner, is as regular a thing in this part of the world as is wine with your meals in France.

Fried hominy is a delicious accompaniment to game, and both rice and hominy form the foundation for many breads and batters, while rice is the backbone of the meat and vegetable pilaus whose name is legion.

TO STIR OR NOT TO STIR?

BOILED RICE

There are many cooks of many minds when it comes to boiling rice. One will tell you never to stir it after it begins to boil or it will be sticky. Another will warn you never to stop stirring it or it will burn. And both of these cooks, if they be real cooks, can turn out the most delectable rice white and fluffy—"with every grain standing apart"—which is the rather alarming way we describe perfectly cooked rice.

But the real trouble is usually found at the bottom— that is, the rice has not been properly washed. This is the most important part of the process. Wash it several times very carefully with cold water, and after you think you have finished, wash it again for luck. Put three cups of water, well salted, in a boiler (an iron pot is always best if you have it) and let it come to a boil.

Then sprinkle the rice in and let it cook briskly for fifteen or twenty minutes, stirring occasionally with a fork. Then pour off the water,[1] or put it in a colander and set it on the back of the stove to steam until dry. Real rice-lovers literally scrape the pot, to get the "rice-cake" at the bottom, but if you haven't been raised on a rice plantation, you won't miss that delectable bit.

Cold rice can be used, as can cold hominy, in breads, battercakes and waffles, or for rice puffs, pilaus, gumbos, croquettes, etc.

BAKED RICE (OR RICE PUFF)

Mix together two cups of cold, boiled rice, one pint of milk, two slightly beaten eggs, three tablespoons of melted butter, and one-half teaspoon of salt. Pour into buttered baking dish, and cook until firm and golden brown.

BOILED HOMINY

It's grist before it is cooked, and hominy afterwards. . . . So, wash your grist in several waters, cover it in the proportion of one part grist to three parts of water, and put it on the stove in a double boiler with salt to taste. Let it boil for one hour or more, stirring frequently to keep from being lumpy.

[1] The servants save this sticky rice-water for starch.

FRIED HOMINY

If you have any hominy left over, spread it out, about one inch or so thick on a platter to get cold. Slice this cold mixture in any shape desired, roll it in eggs and bread crumbs and fry as you would croquettes. It is a very happy accompaniment to birds or game, and a simple addition to breakfast or supper.

BAKED HOMINY (OR HOMINY PUFF)

Mash two cups of cold hominy well to get out the lumps. Add two well-beaten eggs, one large tablespoon of butter, about two cups of milk, and salt to taste. Put in a buttered casserole, and bake in a moderate oven for about forty minutes.

Cooked hominy may be added to batter breads, battercakes, or corn breads with very good results.

MULATTO RICE

This is the very chic name given to rice with a touch of the tarbrush.

Fry squares of breakfast bacon and remove from the pan. Then brown some minced onion (one small one) in this grease, and add one pint can of tomatoes. When thoroughly hot, add a pint of rice to this mixture, and cook very slowly until the rice is done. Or, if you are in a hurry, cold rice may be substituted, and all warmed thoroughly together.

MEXICAN RICE

This seems to be a sort of first cousin to the dark horse above.

Cook a cup of white rice in one pint of strong vegetable stock. Add one tablespoon of chopped green peppers, one peeled tomato, one finely chopped onion, one tablespoon of butter, one-half teaspoon of salt and one-half teaspoon of paprika. Bake in covered dish for two hours.

CURRIED RICE

1 CUP RICE (COOKED SOFT)	1 CUP TOMATOES
1 GREEN PEPPER, CUT UP	4 CUPS WATER
1 LARGE ONION, SLICED	2 TABLESPOONS BUTTER
1½ TEASPOONS CURRY POWDER	

Mix all ingredients and bake in a moderate oven.

PILAUS

Many of the old cooks call pilau "perlew," and we are apt to smile indulgently and explain with raised eyebrows that they mean "pilau," but we would not feel quite so patronizing about it if we realized their authority. In looking over an old South Carolina cook book which specialized on rice dishes, I found this spelled "purlow," so perhaps our admiring imitators are not so far afield after all.

The foundation for all these receipts is breakfast bacon, which is cut into small squares and fried. The bacon is removed and the seasoning cooked in this gravy, then the rice and meat or vegetable (and the bacon) is added. Their name is legion. A few of the most popular ones are given.

TOMATO PILAU

Cut in squares several strips of breakfast bacon, and fry. Remove the bacon from the pan and add two cups of boiled rice and one can of tomatoes. Season to taste, and add the crisp bacon just before serving.

OKRA PILAU

Fry three slices of breakfast bacon, which has been cut in squares. Remove and add two cups of cooked rice and one cup of okra which has been cut and stewed. Simmer together a few minutes, and add the bacon just before serving.

CHICKEN PILAU

Boil one large chicken until very tender. When nearly done, add several strips of bacon, half a dozen small cloves, a small onion, and pepper and salt. When done, take the chicken out, and add two cups of rice to the stock (saving one cup of stock for gravy) and boil until the rice is done.

Put the chicken on a large platter, with rice piled around it, and serve with white sauce made by thickening the remaining stock with a tablespoon of flour and a finely chopped hard boiled egg.

CHICKEN AND TOMATO PILAU

Cut up a fowl and fry it in one tablespoon of lard and one sliced onion. Season one pint can of tomatoes with salt and pepper and one teaspoon of sugar, and when the chicken and onion are a light brown, add the tomatoes and pour boiling water to cover. Have one pint of rice well washed, and stir this into the chicken mixture and simmer until tender. Add one large spoon of butter before serving, and one cup of grated corn can also be added if desired.

RUSSIAN PILAU

1 CUP RAW RICE   1 PINT TOMATOES (CAN OR FRESH)
1 LARGE TABLESPOON BUTTER   1 TEASPOON MINCED ONION
2 CUPS OF COLD MEAT OR SHRIMP OR FISH OR CRABS
SALT AND PEPPER TO TASTE

Wash rice well and drain. Put butter in large frying-pan and when melted cook onion in it until a light brown, then add raw rice and stir constantly in onion and butter until brown, being careful not to burn. Then add tomatoes, one pint of hot water, and when absorbed another pint of boiling water, and cook until rice is tender—about one-half hour. Then add chopped meat or fish and let simmer slowly a few minutes before serving.

ONION RICE

Leave out the tomatoes and the fish, add a little more onion, and proceed as above, and you get a very humble and tasty concoction known as "Onion Rice."

JAMBALAYA

This is in reality our old friend, the pilau, with a more intriguing name, but as this was one of the receipts taught in Mrs. Habersham's famous cooking school, and is a very convenient Monday dish, since any old hang-over from Sunday's dinner seems to be a welcome addition to the brew, it is given a place here.

Put one spoonful of butter in the frying-pan, and add one large cup of cooked rice, one cup of tomato juice or milk, one teaspoon of chopped onion and parsley, and one cup of any kind of vegetable or fish or meat, and stir all together until hot. This is a life saver the day after a party.

WILD RICE WITH MUSHROOMS

Wild Rice is not a native Southern dish, but it has been made a specialty in the Colonial Kitchens, with creamed mushrooms and apple chutney, and the receipt is given here on that account. We cook it as we do native rice, though the directions on the boxes in which it is retailed will tell you to season it more highly. It has a delicious flavor which we think too much seasoning destroys.

Cover one cup of wild rice with about three cups of water and add a little salt. Let it boil hard for about twenty minutes, and when water is absorbed, remove it to the back of the stove and let steam until dry.

Peel one pound of mushrooms, and boil the stems and skins to make stock, which can be strained and used in the creamed mushrooms or put aside for soup. Put two tablespoons of butter in the frying-pan, and broil the mushrooms until a golden brown. Remove and add to the butter, two tablespoons of flour, rubbing it to a smooth paste. Then add a cup of milk (or cream if you are so elegant) and a little mushroom stock, and cook until thick. Add the mushrooms to this, heat thoroughly, and serve on a platter with a border of wild rice.

RICE CROQUETTES

1 LARGE CUP BOILED RICE	½ CUP MILK
1 TABLESPOON BUTTER	1 EGG
NUTMEG—SALT	

Boil milk, add rice and season. When it boils up, add the well-beaten egg, stir well, and let cool. Roll into shapes, roll in bread crumbs, then egg, then bread crumbs again, and fry in deep fat. Delicious with currant jelly.

HOPPING JOHN [1]

This is a great New Year's dish, served with hog's head.

A fine winter's day dinner is a dish of hopping john with roast pork and sweet potatoes.

I PINT COW PEAS   I PINT RICE

I POUND WHITE MEAT

Put peas and meat in about two quarts of water and cook until water is absorbed, then add another pint of water. When this is absorbed, add still another pint and with this put in a pint of rice. Cook until rice is tender, then set on back of stove and steam until dry.

[1] As children, it was our custom, when the word went around that we were to have Hopping John for dinner, to gather in the dining-room, and as the dish was brought on to hop around the table before sitting down to the feast.

CAUTION! All species of marine sea turtles are protected by state and federal laws, most notably the Endangered Species Act of 1973. It is illegal to harm, possess, sell, or transport sea turtles or their shells or eggs. The unauthorized destruction of their habitat is also prohibited.

Gopher tortoises are protected under state laws, including Georgia's, which outlaws the capture, killing, or selling of these animals.

TURTLE EGG HUNT

Turtle eggs are a great delicacy in Savannah, and though they are to be had in quantities when in season, it is quite the thing to go to a great deal of trouble to get them, and a turtle egg hunt on the full of the harvest moon is one of the most popular sports of the late summer season.

The ingredients for this are a moonlight night, a nearby sea-island, and a party of young people to whom time is no object.

After landing on the island, you walk along the beach—en masse or in couples—and if all are not too engrossed, someone eventually discovers a "crawl"—

which being translated means the tracks of Ma turtle, who is on her way from the ocean to attend to her maternal duties, or is returning to the sea, after having performed them. So you follow this crawl along the beach and up into the sand dunes, where you may find the old lady sitting serenely on her nest. It takes the whole party to prize her off, and a part of the technique of a turtle egg hunt from time immemorial is for the party to take turn about riding on her spacious back.

Or you may find that she has covered her newly laid eggs deep in the sand, and returned to the sea, in which case you rob the nest which has been so carefully concealed that it takes a good deal of scratching to find it. There may be anywhere from 60 to 200 eggs—though I have never heard a party report less than the maximum.

TO COOK TURTLE EGGS

And having secured the eggs, the question now before the house is the approved manner of eating them.

They should be cooked about twenty minutes in unsalted water—and opinion differs widely as to the most recherché method of disposing of them after they have been correctly cooked.

One camp holds that anyone who knows what is what simply pinches a little hole in the very elusive shell, inserts a little Worcestershire Sauce and salt into the opening, and bolts the whole thing, much as if it were a bitter dose which should be disposed of as quickly as possible, and about which the less said the better.

Others hold that the whites of the eggs, which never get firm, no matter how long you cook them, were never meant for eating purposes anyhow, and that the correct form is to open the egg, take out the yellow, season it to taste and eat it like a gentleman.

You can pay your money and take your choice.

CAUTION! All species of marine sea turtles are protected by state and federal laws, most notably the Endangered Species Act of 1973. It is illegal to harm, possess, sell, or transport sea turtles or their shells or eggs. The unauthorized destruction of their habitat is also prohibited.

Gopher tortoises are protected under state laws, including Georgia's, which outlaws the capture, killing, or selling of these animals.

VEGETABLES

"AH GOT GREEN CAWN!
AH GOT OKRA!
AH GOT BELL PEPPER!
AH GOT GUINEA SQUASH!"

A newcomer to our shores is often a little surprised at the names to which some of our old vegetables answer. For instance, when we say "Guinea squash," egg plant makes its appearance, and squashes are apt to be listed as "Cimlins." When we say artichokes, we mean, of course, the Jerusalem variety—unless it be a party— then we have "Burr artichokes," meaning the other and more stylish branch of the family, though I have never seen that name in any of the cook books. The colored people are apt to call butter beans "see-wee" or "civvy" beans, but this seems to have a foundation in fact, since the dictionary opines that a lima bean (which is a large variety of our butter bean) is also known as the Siveau or Civet Bean.

OKRA

Take young tender okra pods, cut off ends, and boil in salted water about twenty minutes. Drain. add pepper and salt and butter, and let simmer on stove a few minutes before serving.

OKRA AND TOMATOES

1 PINT OKRA   1 PINT TOMATOES

Cut up okra, peel tomatoes. Put in saucepan without water, and add a teaspoon of sugar, a chopped onion, a little salt and pepper, and stew together fifteen minutes.

BAKED SQUASH

Peel and remove cores from two pounds of summer squash. Boil in salted water fifteen minutes. Drain and mash through colander. Add one cup of bread crumbs, salt, pepper, a little onion juice (broiled in two tablespoons melted butter). Put in deep dish or buttered pan, sprinkle bread crumbs on top and brown.

"BUTTON" SQUASH

The little round white or "button" squash are delightful served whole with drawn butter or white sauce. To prepare them, wash carefully, take out core, and cook in salted water about fifteen minutes.

SHOE STRING ONIONS

Take a large, white, Bermuda onion, and slice into pieces about one-eighth inch thick. Soak several hours in iced water, and when ready to cook, drain well, salt, and roll in flour. Fry in deep fat until a golden brown. A delicious and delicate dish for luncheon or supper.

STUFFED EGG PLANT

Select two medium sized egg plants and, after washing, dry and cut into halves lengthwise. Scoop out meat, leaving the rind thick enough to keep shape. Chop the meat fine, mix with bread crumbs (about equal quantity), two tablespoons of melted butter, salt and pepper (a little chopped onion and bell pepper give additional flavor if desired). Moisten with brown stock, fill the shells, place a strip of bacon on top of each, place in buttered pan and bake for thirty-five or forty minutes.

BAKED EGG PLANT

Cook two egg plants in boiling water, drain, cool and peel. Put through colander and add one cup of bread crumbs, two eggs, a little bell pepper, two teaspoons of chopped onion, two tablespoons of butter, and salt to taste. Put in deep dish, cover with bread crumbs and brown.

EGG PLANT SOUFFLÉ

Cut two large egg plants into slices. Boil in salted water, peel and mash. To three cups of egg plant, add one tablespoon of butter, two eggs beaten lightly, one-half cup of milk, one-half teaspoon of salt, dash of pepper, one cup of bread crumbs, and one cup of grated cheese. Put in baking dish, sprinkle bread crumbs on top and cook about fifteen minutes.

SPINACH SOUFFLÉ

To two cups of cooked spinach, which have been put through a colander, add cream sauce made of two tablespoons of butter, two of flour, one cup of milk and one cup of grated cheese. Mix well and cool, then add the well-beaten whites of three eggs. Put in buttered dish and cook fifteen or twenty minutes.

TOMATOES AND BELL PEPPERS

Chop one bell pepper and one piece of celery in small pieces, and cook a few minutes in three tablespoons of melted butter. Add one quart of tomatoes, two cups of bread crumbs, one tablespoon of sugar, salt and pepper, and put in deep pan. Sprinkle with bread crumbs and bake about one-half hour.

CORN CREOLE

1 CUP CANNED CORN

1 CUP WELL SEASONED TOMATO SAUCE

1 RED OR GREEN PEPPER, CUT UP

Stew all together a few minutes, and serve on toast. A simple and savory luncheon dish.

CORN PUDDING

Mix together one quart of fresh corn, scraped or grated, three cups of milk, three well-beaten eggs, three tablespoons of sifted flour, three tablespoons of butter, salt and pepper to taste, and pour in well-buttered deep pan. Bake in moderate oven for one hour.

CORN FRITTERS

1 CAN CORN	4 TABLESPOONS FLOUR
2 EGGS	1 TABLESPOON BAKING POWDER
1 TEASPOON SALT	1 TABLESPOON SUGAR

Beat all together, and drop one tablespoon at a time, into deep fat. This makes an innumerable number of delicious fritters.

JERUSALEM ARTICHOKES

Scrape or peel artichokes. Let your conscience be your guide—they are better scraped! Throw them into cold water to keep from turning dark. Cook in salted, boiling water until tender, and serve with drawn butter. A delicate and most delicious vegetable.

CREAMED CABBAGE

Shred a small white cabbage, and plunge a handful at a time into salted boiling water. As soon as it boils up once, drain, and serve with a white sauce made of one tablespoon of butter, one tablespoon of flour and a cup of milk. Fine, and a very inexpensive dish to serve in a hurry.

MACARONI CROQUETTES

Cook one cup of macaroni in salted, boiling water until tender. Drain, and stir into it a cream sauce made of two tablespoons butter, one tablespoon flour and one cup of milk. Add one-half teaspoon of salt, one-half cup of grated cheese, and let cool. Then mold into shapes, roll in eggs and bread crumbs and fry in deep fat.

PALMETTO CABBAGE
(or Hearts of Palmetto)

The Carolina Housewife, long out of print, gives this receipt for a great delicacy. The "cabbage" or heart of the palmetto tree is an ivory-like substance which is occasionally offered for sale when palmetto groves have been cleared away. But it is a rare delicacy, and eating fresh hearts of palmettoes is in the class with dining on pheasants' tongues.

The cabbage or heart must be trimmed and only the very tender part used. It must be boiled for two hours, during which time the water must be changed three times, so that the bitter quality will be extracted. When quite soft, pour off water, and mash with wooden or silver spoon. Add one large tablespoon of fresh butter, a little salt and pepper, and reheat with a gill of cream. Or it may be served cold as a salad with French dressing.

OKRA FRITTERS

Boil one quart of okra. Strain off water and mash. Season with salt and pepper, beat in two eggs, two teaspoons of baking powder, and enough flour to make a stiff batter. Drop one tablespoonful at a time in deep fat and fry.

ASPARAGUS SOUFFLÉ

1 CAN ASPARAGUS (DARK GREEN VARIETY)	3 EGGS
2 CUPS BREADCRUMBS	2 CUPS MILK
1 TABLESPOON BUTTER	SALT AND PEPPER

Beat eggs with salt and pepper until light. Add asparagus (cut up), bread crumbs and milk. Pour into buttered dish and bake in a pan of hot water twenty minutes.

BROCCOLI

Trim off leaves and cut off tough parts of stem. Have ready two quarts of boiling, salted, water. Put in broccoli with a pinch of soda, and cook hard for ten or fifteen minutes. Remove from water and serve immediately with drawn butter sauce. If a large quantity of broccoli is to be cooked, it is a good idea to tie several heads together, and great care should be taken in removing from pot so as not to break stalks.

Hollandaise is a popular sauce with this vegetable, but the flavor of broccoli is so delicate that many prefer the drawn butter.

Cold broccoli with French dressing is a delicious salad.

CANDIED SWEET POTATOES

This is by far the most popular way of serving this plentiful winter vegetable, and most of the receipts direct you to bake it in a pan with sugar, and water, and some particular flavoring, such as lemon or cinnamon, and occasionally it is embellished with marshmallows. But the following receipt is much simpler, and far, far nicer, since all of the potatoes get thoroughly candied in this process, and never dry out in the baking.

Make a syrup of one pint of water, one pound of sugar, butter the size of an egg and a little nutmeg. Peel eight or ten raw potatoes, slice and drop into this syrup. Cover and boil slowly until well done. The potatoes will be clear and thoroughly candied—and altogether heavenly.

MORE CANDIED SWEET POTATOES

The other method—and the usual one—if you prefer it, is like this. Boil several large sweet potatoes. Peel, and cut in slices. Fill bottom of baking pan with a layer of potatoes, sprinkle with a tablespoon of sugar and a small lump of butter. Add another layer of potatoes, another spoon of sugar, another lump of butter, and so on to the top. Put in a few slices of lemon, cover well with cold water, and bake until potatoes are candied.

YAMS

The large yellow yam is more often baked in its own skin, and eaten hot with butter. The name "yam" is supposed to be a contraction of the gullah word "nyam", which means to eat.

Samuel Stoney in *Black Genesis,* traces it to the African word, "unyamo," which has dropped the first and last syllable. He also says that the negroes call the white, or Irish, potato "buckra yam," buckra in gullah meaning white man.

CREAMED SWEET POTATOES

2 CUPS COOKED AND MASHED POTATOES

½ TEASPOON CINNAMON	1 CUP MILK
½ CUP SUGAR	½ CUP SEEDED RAISINS

BUTTER SIZE OF AN EGG

Beat all together until light and fluffy, and cook in buttered baking dish. Remove and sprinkle marshmallows on top, return to oven and brown.

Personally, I think the last item should be honored in the breach rather than in the observance, but if you like the marshmallow touch, you might even go a step further, by stuffing the mixture into hollowed-out orange skins, decorating the individual dishes with a few marshmallows and running them in the oven before serving. It tastes fine, but rather raises it out of the vegetable class—and then, what have you?

SWEET POTATO CROQUETTES

Mash one large, boiled sweet potato, add a little sugar, a pinch of salt, two tablespoons of butter, and one slightly beaten egg. Shape into croquettes, roll in flour, and fry in deep fat. Or they may be rolled into little balls, instead of the elongated croquette, and fried in the same manner.

SWEET POTATO SNOW BALLS

Blend two cups of mashed, cooked, sweet potatoes with one-half cup of brown sugar, one tablespoon of butter and one-half teaspoon of ground spice. Take ten marshmallows, and roll each separately into this mixture, forming balls. Then roll these balls in shredded cocoanut, place in oven and cook long enough for the marshmallows to heat but not melt.

SWEET POTATO PONE

1 QUART GRATED POTATO	¾ POUND SUGAR
¾ POUND BUTTER	½ PINT MILK

1 TABLESPOON POWDERED GINGER

GRATED PEEL OF ONE SWEET ORANGE

Rub ingredients well together and bake in a shallow plate in a slow oven. A little molasses may be added.

In the northern part of the state, where the frost sweetens the persimmons in the fall, a delicious touch is given the potato pone by adding a cup or more of persimmons before cooking.

FRIED SWEET POTATOES

An old-fashioned breakfast dish, when breakfast was something to be reckoned with, was fried sweet potatoes.

Peel and slice the raw potatoes, sprinkle with salt and fry in hot fat.

Cold boiled sweet potatoes, left-over candied potatoes, may also be fried in this fashion, and make a nice luncheon dish.

SWEET POTATO MERINGUE

6 POTATOES	I TABLESPOON SUGAR
2 EGGS	¼ CUP MILK
SALT TO TASTE	

Boil potatoes until tender, peel and mash. Add sugar, milk, yolks of eggs and salt. Beat hard until mixture is light and creamy. Put in dish and bake one-half hour. Take out and spread well-beaten whites on top. Return to oven and brown.

HASHED POTATOES (IRISH)

Fry a dessert spoon of chopped onion in a little butter. Sift in a dessert spoon of flour, another spoon of

butter, salt and pepper, and one cup of milk. Let boil
until it coats the spoon. Add to this a cup of cooked
and diced potatoes. Heat well and serve.

POTATO CROQUETTES

2 CUPS COOKED IRISH POTATOES

2 TABLESPOONS BUTTER   I EGG

SALT TO TASTE

Mash potatoes while hot, and mix with eggs, butter
and salt, and put aside to cool. When firm, roll into
croquettes and fry in deep fat. Do NOT roll in bread
crumbs.

IRISH POTATO PIE

Use any kind of cooked meat, cut into dice. Line a
deep dish with cooked and mashed and salted potatoes,
then put in meat and small bits of butter, and one cup
of gravy, if you have it. Cover with potatoes and bake
fifteen minutes. One of those life-savers, when there is
"nothing in the house."

POT POURRI: SAUCES, DRESSINGS, HORS D'ŒUVRES

POT POURRI

SAUCES, DRESSINGS, SUGGESTIONS FOR HORS D'ŒUVRES AND WHAT HAVE YOU?

COCKTAIL SAUCE

A most delectable cocktail sauce for shrimp is made by adding to one cup of mayonnaise about one-half cup of chili sauce. Have this thoroughly chilled, and just before serving, thin it out with a little cream. Marvelous!

* * * *

SAUCE FOR GAME

One stick broken cinnamon, a little lemon peel, one and one-half glasses of port, one tablespoon of brown sugar, a few cloves and one-half glass of currant jelly. Put spices, lemon, sugar and wine in saucepan to heat, not boil. Strain this over jelly, and let boil up once before serving.

* * * *

APPLE BALL SAUCE FOR GOOSE

Peel apples and cut into little balls with potato cutter. Make syrup of one cup sugar, three quarters of a cup of water, two cloves and several thin shavings of lemon. Cook seven minutes, removing cloves and lemon peel. Put apples in and cook until tender.

* * * *

HOT DRESSING FOR GAME

Rub together a heaping tablespoon of butter, one tablespoon of flour, and add one-half pint of broth (or canned bouillon, if you are more modern), one teaspoon of mushrooms, a little Worcestershire Sauce, two teaspoons of lemon juice, and two tablespoons of cream. Put in double boiler, and stir in slightly beaten yolks of two eggs. Stew together but do not boil.

* * * *

SAUCE FOR FISH

A wonderful sauce for fish is made by mixing together one tablespoon of Worcestershire Sauce, one tablespoon of Tarragon vinegar, one tablespoon of lemon juice, two tablespoons of butter, and salt and pepper to taste.

* * * *

SAUCE FOR MUTTON OR LAMB

Warm together a tablespoon of Worcestershire Sauce, two tablespoons of wine, one teaspoon of butter, one teaspoon of mustard, salt and pepper to taste, and a little gravy in which the meat has been cooked.

A DELICIOUS FRENCH DRESSING FOR FRUIT SALAD OR TOMATOES

To one-half cup of confectioners' sugar, add two teaspoons of paprika, four tablespoons of lemon juice, two teaspoons of salt, and stir in slowly one cup of olive oil. It should be almost the consistency of mayonnaise.

*　　*　　*　　*

SHRIMP SAUCE FOR FISH

Grind up one dozen shrimp, and mix with one cup of drawn butter, one spoon of vinegar, and salt and pepper to taste. Boil up once and serve.

*　　*　　*　　*

CURRY DRESSING FOR ENDIVE

Mix one-quarter teaspoon of salt, one teaspoon of curry powder, with one tablespoon of vinegar, and stir in one-quater cup of olive oil.

*　　*　　*　　*

PECAN STUFFING FOR TURKEY

Shell pecans and put through grinder. Mix with enough bread crumbs to hold them together, and season with melted butter, pepper, salt, and a suspicion of chopped onion.

SAUCE FOR SPINACH

A little brown sugar, a very little dry mustard, cayenne pepper, salt, and one well-beaten egg. Mix well in a little boiling vinegar.

* * * *

DRESSING FOR SHRIMP SALAD

If you add chopped celery and pimentos to the mayonnaise you use for shrimp salad, it will taste like lobster.

* * * *

DRESSING FOR CRAB SALAD

Use one part Worcestershire Sauce to two parts mayonnaise for a distinctive dressing for crab salad.

* * * *

TOMATO SALAD DRESSING

Into a quart jar put the following ingredients in the order given.

One can of tomato soup, three-quarters of a cup of vinegar, one-half cup of oil, one-fourth cup of sugar, a tablespoon of Worcestershire Sauce, and three tablespoons of grated onion.

Mix together one teaspoon of salt, one scant teaspoon mustard and one teaspoon paprika, and add this to ingredients in jar. Seal, shake well, and put in refrigerator. It will keep indefinitely.

A TOUCH OF GREEN

No salads are included in this book, because they are not especially Southern, and because we agree with the French that nothing can improve the simple method of marinating with good dressing lettuce, escarole or endive, and letting it go at that. Adding anything to this is but painting the lily.

Given a head of lettuce and a dash of imagination, a salad may be made from anything in the vegetable kingdom, and receipts for them are legion.

DRESSING FOR COLE SLAW

2 EGGS	½ CUP SUGAR
½ TEASPOON SALT	PINCH CAYENNE
¼ TEASPOON DRY MUSTARD	½ CUP VINEGAR
I SMALL TEASPOON CORNSTARCH	LUMP OF BUTTER

Mix all ingredients and cook slowly in double boiler. Thin it with a little cream or milk.

The cabbage should be shredded and plunged in iced water, then dried before mixing with the dressing.

TWO SIMPLE RELISHES

A substantial and very tasty hors d'œuvre is made thus: Cut slices of bread in round shapes and toast a light brown. Spread each with anchovy paste, and put a slice of toast on each plate. On each slice of toast, a slice of tomato, on each tomato, a half of a hard-boiled egg, and over all pour mayonnaise which has been thinned out with plenty of lemon.

Another tasty relish, which may be served with the cocktails, or in place of them as the case may be, is made with the humble peanut butter.

Cut each slice of sandwich bread into four small squares, and cover each square with peanut butter. Top each with a small piece of breakfast bacon, and run them in the oven at the last moment to toast quickly. Better make plenty, as your guests will eat more than you thought possible.

SWEETBREAD COQUILLES

Take two pairs of sweetbreads (will make enough for six persons), parboil, and cut in small pieces. Chop a can of mushrooms very fine, cook in their own liquor, drain, and add to the sweetbreads. Season with salt, pepper, nutmeg, a little lemon juice, and two sprigs of parsley chopped fine. Heat two cups of milk in a double boiler, rub a little butter into flour, mix into one well-beaten egg and stir slowly into the boiling milk. Pour this mixture over the seasoned sweetbreads and serve.

HOME MADE "PÂTÉ DE FOIE GRAS"

Boil a calf's liver until very tender in water that has been slightly salted, and in another vessel a calf's tongue. It is best to do this the day before making the pâté, as they should be cold and firm.

Cut the liver into bits, and rub them smoothly to a paste, moistening as you go along with salted butter. Work into this paste one-quarter teaspoon of cayenne, one-half of a grated nutmeg, a little cloves, a teaspoon of Worcestershire Sauce, salt to taste, one teaspoon of mustard and a tablespoon of boiling water in which a minced onion has been steeped until the flavor is extracted. Work all well together and pack in jars. Butter the inside of the jars well, and pack the pâté very hard, inserting here and there bits of the tongue. Cover jars with melted butter. It will last a long time.

SOUFFLÉ

Make one cup of cream sauce, and while hot stir in one cup of finely chopped meat or cheese. Beat separately the yolks and whites of two eggs. Stir yolks into the sauce mixture, let cook one minute and remove from stove. When cool, stir in the stiffly beaten whites, bake in oven twenty minutes, and serve immediately.

DID YOU KNOW THAT

The secret of good seasoning is garlic—but that you will be sorry if you take that too seriously?

That aspic made from the juice of pickled peaches or other fruit is an excellent accompaniment for cold meats? One pint of juice to one tablespoon (or one-half package) of gelatine is the proportion?

That the juice from pickled fruits also makes a delicious spiced French dressing?

That the juice from brandied peaches makes a perfect cocktail sauce for any kind of fruit?

That mushroom sauce turns warmed-over lamb or veal into something to write home about?

That if you put a little salt in the whipped cream which you serve on creamed soups, and add a little cut-up parsley, it will make it additionally attractive?

That a little baking powder in your meringues will keep them from falling?

That brown sugar is better than white for all kinds of punch stock, since it makes a thicker syrup, and that some people go so far as to say you should always use it for strawberry sauce?

That cole slaw is a fine accompaniment for fish, if you have no cucumbers?

That shredded lettuce makes a delightful garnish?

DESSERTS

"STRAWBERRY—GEORGIA STRAW!"

Syllabub and Ambrosia always marked red letter days in my childhood, and were invariably the signs of company to dinner—so they shall headline the lists of desserts, although one seldom meets them nowadays. Here's hoping for a revival of those simple and delectable dishes!

SYLLABUB

To one pint of cream add a gill of white wine, the grated rind of one lemon, the whites of three eggs and four tablespoons of powdered sugar. Whip until stiff, turn in to sherbet glasses and chill.

AMBROSIA

A layer of sliced oranges, a layer of shredded fresh cocoanut, a layer of sugar, and so on, ad infinitum, depending on the size of your dish and your company. What could be simpler, and more delicious?

Of course, if a little wine could be poured over all, it would be so much the better.

CHARLOTTE RUSSE

1 TABLESPOON GELATINE	1 CUP MILK
1 PINT CREAM	½ PINT SUGAR
WHITES 4 EGGS	VANILLA—OR BETTER IF POSSIBLE

Soak the gelatine in a little cold water, and dissolve in warm milk. When cold, add the cream, well-whipped, the sugar, and, lastly, the stiffly beaten egg whites and flavoring.

STRAWBERRY SHORT CAKE

Make a rich pie crust of one pint of flour, one teaspoon baking powder, one tablespoon of butter or lard, roll out thin and bake in pie pan. When done, split with sharp knife, butter well, and spread between a strawberry mixture made of one quart of strawberries mashed with one cup of sugar. Spread another layer of the mixture on top, and serve warm with whipped cream, slightly sweetened.

APPLE MERINGUE

Sweeten to taste two cups of stewed apples, and flavor with a teaspoon of vanilla. Put in baking dish and cover with a stiff meringue made of the whites of two eggs whipped up with nearly a cup of sugar (not powdered), and another teaspoon of vanilla. Bake until the meringue is a light brown. The well-beaten yolks of the two eggs may be added to the apple mixture, if desired, before the meringue is put on, but it is a little more delicate, though not so rich, without it. Serve cold with cream. Delicious.

MOONSHINE

is a very simple hot weather dessert. Beat the whites of six eggs with two cups of sugar until very stiff, then fold in a heaping tablespoon of preserved fruit or jelly. Set on ice to chill thoroughly, and serve with cream.

ORANGE SOUFFLÉ

Dissolve one-half box of gelatine in one-half cup of cold water. Add to one pint of orange juice the yolks of six eggs and one pound of sugar. Beat well together. Place bowl in a larger vessel of cracked ice, and stir the mixture until it begins to thicken, then add one pint of whipped cream, and put it all into the Frigidaire, or pack in ice and salt.

MARRON MOUSSE

3 EGGS	I SCANT CUP SUGAR
I PINT CREAM	I CAN MARRONS
LADY FINGERS	

Whip whites of eggs stiff—ditto the yolks with sugar. Whip cream and flavor with juice from marrons. Line mold with lady fingers and marrons, pour in the mixture and freeze three hours.

PEACH MOUSSE

Mash one can of peaches through colander, and sweeten with one cup sugar. Add one teaspoon of lemon juice and a little almond extract. Heat the juice from the can and pour it over two tablespoons of gelatine which have been soaked in a little cold water. Cool and mix with the fruit pulp. Put in mold, and when firm serve with whipped cream.

PINEAPPLE CHARLOTTE

A simple and very good dessert is made by lining sherbet glasses with lady fingers, and filling with a mixture made of pineapple cut in blocks and mixed with sweetened whipped cream. Chill and serve.

QUICK, HOT WEATHER DESSERT

To the yolks of three eggs, beaten light, add gradually two-thirds cup of sugar and grated rind of one-half a lemon. Soak a tablespoon of gelatine in a little water, and melt in hot water. Add four tablespoons of lemon juice and stir into the egg mixture. Then add well-beaten whites. Chill and serve with slightly sweetened whipped cream.

TIPSY SQUIRE

Put sponge cake in the bottom of a deep dish. Blanch and split half a pound of almonds, and stick about in the cake. Mix in a tumbler some sherry wine and water, and sweeten to taste. Pour this over the cake. Make a custard of one quart of milk and six eggs, and pour over this.

SPANISH CREAM

Mix three cups of scalded milk with one tablespoon of gelatine, previously soaked in a little water. Add a scant half-cup of sugar. Pour this slowly on the well-beaten yolks of three eggs, return to double boiler and cook until thick, stirring constantly. Remove from range, and add one-fourth teaspoon of salt, one teaspoon vanilla (or three tablespoons of wine) and beaten whites of three eggs. Turn into individual molds, first dipped into cold water, and chill. Serve with slightly sweetened whipped cream.

BURNT CREAM

¾ CUP SUGAR	1 PINT MILK
YOLK 1 EGG	1 ½ TABLESPOONS CORNSTARCH

Caramelize the sugar in a little water on the stove. Heat milk and stir into the melted sugar. Rub the cornstarch smooth in a little cold milk and add to the yolk of the eggs, well beaten. Add this to the milk and sugar mixture, and cook until thick. Let cool, and before serving, cover with whipped cream and ground burnt almonds.

TYLER PUDDING

This receipt belonged to President Tyler's family, and was given by Miss Mary Lee Tyler to a friend in Hay Market, Virginia, many years ago.

Put in a double boiler:

1½ CUPS GRANULATED SUGAR	1½ CUPS BROWN SUGAR
1 CUP HEAVY CREAM	YOLKS 4 EGGS
¾ CUP OF BUTTER	

Cook until thick and add vanilla and the well-beaten egg whites. Pour into pans which have been lined with rich pastry, and sprinkle with nutmeg. Bake in a moderate oven until custard is set. If it does not get thick enough in the cooking, add a little cornstarch.

This is to be served very cold, and is excellent with vanilla ice cream. Rich? Of course, but was it not presidential fare?

SERENE PUDDING

1 PINT MILK	1 CUP SUGAR
A LITTLE SALT	4 EGGS
⅓ BOX OF GELATINE	

Cook milk, sugar, the yolks of eggs and salt together until it begins to boil. Then add the gelatine, which has been soaked in three-quarters cup of cold water. When cold, stir in the well-beaten egg whites, add vanilla, and let congeal.

BATTER PUDDING

One quart of milk, five eggs, five level tablespoons of flour. Beat eggs separately, work the yolks and flour together, and add milk slowly until thoroughly mixed. Add whites beaten stiff. Grease baking dish, and bake until pudding is set, and a golden brown.

CHOCOLATE PUDDING

¼ CUP BUTTER	½ CUP SUGAR
½ CUP MILK	1⅓ CUPS FLOUR
1½ TEASPOONS BAKING POWDER	1 EGG
1 SQUARE MELTED CHOCOLATE	½ TEASPOON VANILLA

Cream butter and sugar and add well-beaten yolks of eggs. Then stir in, alternately, milk and flour. Set aside until ready to bake. Then stir in baking powder and melted chocolate, vanilla and well-beaten whites of eggs. Bake in a ring, and serve cold with whipped cream in the center, and hot chocolate sauce.

BLACKBERRY PUDDING

Mix six tablespoons of flour gradually in one pint of milk, and stir in a little salt, one egg, the yolks and whites beaten separately, and one quart of blackberries. Cook this mixture on top of stove until it begins to thicken, then put in buttered dish and bake for one-half hour. Serve with hard sauce.

CARAMEL CUSTARD

3 EGGS	I TABLESPOON WATER
I CUP BROWN SUGAR	I PINT SCALDED MILK
	TEASPOON VANILLA

Melt sugar and water, stirring constantly, and add boiling milk. Add eggs and flavoring and bake in buttered dish in quick oven. Serve cold.

MARIE LOUISE ICE CREAM

Make a strong, stiff, very sweet wine jelly as follows: Soak one envelope of gelatine in one-half cup of cold water, and dissolve in one cup of boiling water. Add one and one-half cups of sugar. When cold add two cups of sherry, and set aside to get firm. Break jelly into small pieces with fork, and add one pint of cream whipped stiff. Mix thoroughly, put in mold which has been dipped in cold water, pack in salt and ice for three or four hours.

FIG AND PEACH ICE CREAM

Mix one pint of custard and one pint of cream and freeze. When half frozen add one large cup of peaches, and one large cup of figs, which have been mashed through the colander, and finish freezing.

ICE BOX CAKE

Melt three squares of Baker's chocolate. Beat the yolks of nine eggs until creamy, add one cup of sugar, and pour the hot chocolate into this. Then add the well-beaten whites of the eggs, and one-half cup of powdered sugar and a teaspoon of vanilla.

Line a mold with lady fingers, pour in this mixture and let stand several hours. Serve with whipped cream.

PECAN PIE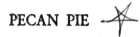

4 EGGS	1½ CUPS KARO SYRUP (RED LABEL)
1 CUP SUGAR	½ CUP SHELLED PECANS
1 TABLESPOON BUTTER	PINCH OF SALT
1 TEASPOONFUL VANILLA	

Beat eggs and mix with all ingredients. Line pan with pastry, pour in the mixture and bake one hour.

RICE CUSTARD

1 CUP RICE	1 PINT MILK
½ CUP BUTTER	3 EGGS
RAISINS AND CURRANTS	

Boil rice and strain, or use cooked rice which has been left over. Add milk and butter and eggs, slightly beaten. Sweeten and flavor to taste, put in a deep dish and bake. When half done, stir in raisins and currants. If these are put in at first they will settle on bottom.

PARFAIT D'AMOUR

Put some peach ice cream in a glass, pour over it a tablespoon of raspberry or fruit syrup, and let it trickle through. Then add a tablespoon of whipped cream and serve.

MERINGUES

One-quarter cup of sugar to each white of egg and a pinch of salt is a good proportion for a stiff meringue. Beat until it hurts, if by hand, or until it is stiff enough to stand alone.

For a large meringue, drop one and one-half tablespoons at a time on a pan lined with well-buttered brown paper, and cook from twenty minutes to one-half hour in a very slow oven. It is a good idea to put them in a cold stove, and let it heat gradually, as they should literally dry out, not cook. When nearly done, scoop out soft centers, leaving the shell to be filled with ice cream or any cream dessert, and dry these out again in the oven.

ALMOND CREAM FILLING

A delicious almond and cream filling is made by mixing one cup of whipped cream with one-half cup of sugar and one pound of almonds, blanched and chopped fine.

ELIZA'S DESSERT

One pint of cream, one-half pound of marshmallows, each cut in four pieces, one teaspoon of vanilla. Beat until stiff.

Add one large cup of pecans, and one small cup of Maraschino cherries, one-half dozen kisses, or lady fingers, broken up, and put on ice.

PEACH CREAM

Twelve peaches peeled, stoned, and cut in halves, three eggs, and the white of one more, one-half cup of powdered sugar, two tablespoons of cornstarch moistened with a little cold milk, one tablespoon of melted butter, and one pint of milk.

Scald milk, stir in cornstarch, and take from fire when it begins to thicken. Stir in the butter. When lukewarm, whip in the beaten yolks until all is very light.

Put a thick layer of peaches into a baking dish, strew thickly with sugar, and pour the cream compound over all. Bake in a quick oven ten minutes. Cover with a meringue made of the whites of four eggs whipped stiff with a little powdered sugar. Brown slightly.

BREAD PUDDING

Beat together the yolks of four eggs and one-quarter cup of sugar. Pour this mixture into one pint of hot milk, add a pinch of salt, one-half teaspoon of vanilla and one-half teaspoon of almond extract.

Put into a baking dish, or individual ramikins. Butter slices of stale bread, put on top of custard, buttered side up, and cook in a pan of hot water about fifteen minutes.

This is delicious served with caramel sauce.

UPSIDE DOWN PINEAPPLE CAKE

1 CUP BUTTER	½ CUP SUGAR
1 CUP FLOUR	2 EGGS
2 TEASPOONS BAKING POWDER	½ CUP MILK

Cream together the butter and sugar, add the eggs, then the milk and flour, alternately (the baking powder having been sifted with the flour). Put in the bottom of a cake pan, two tablespoons of butter, one cup of brown sugar and melt. Then lay on this the cut-up fruit from one can of pineapple, and pour the cake batter over this. Bake about twenty minutes, and turn upside down on cake platter. Serve with whipped cream.

SOFT CUSTARD

1 QUART MILK	1 SCANT TEACUP SUGAR
½ TEASPOON SALT	YOLKS 8 EGGS

WHITES 2 EGGS

1 TEASPOON VANILLA OR LEMON OR ½ TEASPOON ALMOND EXTRACT

Beat sugar and egg and add one cup of the milk. Let rest of milk boil and pour into it the beaten mixture.

Put in double boiler and cook, stirring constantly, until thick. Then add salt and cool. Then add flavoring.

The rest of the egg whites beaten, and slightly sweetened, may be used on top as a meringue.

BROWN BETTY

2 CUPS APPLES, PEELED AND SLICED

½ CUP SUGAR   2 TABLESPOONS BUTTER

1 TEASPOON CINNAMON   TOASTED OR VERY STALE BREAD

Line a buttered pan with a layer of apples, then a layer of toasted or stale bread, sprinkle with sugar and a little cinnamon, and small pieces of butter, and repeat until the pan is full. Cover pan so it will steam, and bake in oven about three-quarters of an hour. Then remove cover and allow to brown. Serve with hard sauce.

LEMON CHEESE FILLING FOR CAKES AND PIES

This is a very old receipt, and as the mixture will keep indefinitely, it is a wonderful thing to have on tap.

1 POUND SUGAR   6 EGGS

¼ POUND BUTTER   GRATED RIND 2 LEMONS

JUICE OF 3 LEMONS

Put all together in a double boiler, and cook slowly over fire until the consistency of custard.

CAKES

ANGEL FOOD CAKE

is all that the name implies, and is as difficult of accomplishment as any other angelic performance. Only practice makes perfect. You cannot attain it by the hit and miss method, as you can so many other things, but it is the easiest thing in all the world to eat when once it is well made.

To begin with, an expert cake maker—a cordon bleu in whom we all have implicit faith—tells me that she *measures* the whites of the eggs instead of counting them, since they are so temperamental as to size, and temperamentality does not go in Angel Cake.

Wherefore:

1 ¼ CUPS OF EGG WHITES	1 CUP FLOUR
1 ½ CUPS SUGAR	1 TEASPOON CREAM OF TARTAR
1 TEASPOON VANILLA	PINCH SALT

BERY WELL, DEN! LET'S GO. . . .

Put the salt and cream of tartar in the whites of the eggs, and beat until stiff—but not too stiff, or the cake will be tough. Then put the sugar in, a tablespoon at a time, still beating until it "peaks," and very slowly add the flour, then the vanilla, and put in a deep ungreased pan. Cook slowly, and when done, turn pan upside down, and do not touch until cold. Then cut around the sides of the pan with a knife to "disengage" it, as the old cook books say,—and here's hoping it will be Angel's Food indeed.

And you've saved milk by this expensive layout!

SPONGE CAKE

This sponge cake is famous in Savannah, and the proportions given here make two large cakes. It seems enormous, so, if you think your family will be satisfied with one, divide the proportions in half—and then have it all to do over again a few days later!

10 EGGS   1 POUND GRANULATED SUGAR
½ POUND SWANSDOWN FLOUR
                          JUICE AND RIND OF 2 LEMONS

The art is in the making, so follow the directions verbatim.

Separate eggs and put the yolks in a large bowl, and the whites on a large platter.

Grate the rind of the lemons and set aside in the strained juice to "steep."

Sift the flour three times.

Grease two large "stove-pipe" pans, and then proceed.

Beat the egg yolks until *very* light, adding sugar gradually, then the lemon juice and peel.

Beat the whites until stiff and dry. The old-fashioned flat egg beater is highly recommended instead of the Doyer beater or the more new-fangled electric life savers, as it makes the eggs dryer. You'll get stiff and dry before they do, but no matter. . . .

Stir the beaten whites into the beaten yolks, and into this custard-like mixture sift again the already thrice-sifted flour, folding it in very lightly.

Divide the batter in half, and bake in two pans in a *slow* oven for about forty-five minutes.

Extravagant? Perhaps . . . but think of the butter and baking powder you save by making it!

LADY BALTIMORE CAKE

(Which of course is THE *one which Owen Wister made famous)*

1 CUP BUTTER	1 CUP SUGAR	1 CUP MILK
3½ CUPS FLOUR	2 TEASPOONS BAKING POWDER	
1 TEASPOON VANILLA	6 EGGS—WHITES ONLY	

Cream the butter and sugar, add gradually the milk and flour (in which the baking powder has been sifted) and lastly the well-beaten egg whites. Bake in shallow tins, and put this filling between the layers—the filling is what made the cake famous.

Three cups of sugar boiled with one cup of water until stringy. Pour this over the well-beaten whites of three eggs, and add one cup of chopped pecans, one cup of seeded raisins and one-half cup of chopped figs.

CREAM CAKE

1 PINT FLOUR	1 CUP SUGAR	½ CUP BUTTER
2 EGGS	2 TEASPOONS BAKING POWDER	
	1 CUP OF MILK AND WATER MIXED	

Cream the butter and sugar, add the eggs (unbeaten) and the flour and milk, and vanilla if desired. Bake in two layers, and put between them the following filling:

Mix together one pint of milk, four even tablespoons of sugar, one egg, two tablespoons of flour (moistened in a little cold milk), and cook until very thick. Put aside to cool, and when cool spread between layers of cake, and serve with cream.

ONE-TWO-THREE CAKE

The batter for the famous one-two-three cake, which is the foundation for all simple layer or individual cakes, is made of one cup of butter, two of sugar, three of flour (with three teaspoons of baking powder) four eggs and enough milk or water to make the batter the right consistency.

Cream the butter and sugar, add the egg yolks, then, alternately, the milk and flour, and lastly the whites of eggs and flavoring.

SOUR CREAM GINGER CAKE

1 CUP SOUR CREAM	1 CUP BLACK MOLASSES
2 CUPS FLOUR	1 TEASPOON GINGER
1 TEASPOON SODA	PINCH SALT

Mix molasses and cream, and add flour, soda and salt, and beat until well mixed. This should be about the consistency of cake dough, and milk or flour may be added if necessary. Bake slowly about one hour and serve with whipped cream.

DOLLY VARDEN CAKE

⅔ CUP BUTTER   2 CUPS SUGAR   1 CUP MILK

3 CUPS FLOUR   3 EGGS   2 TEASPOONS BAKING POWDER

FLAVORING

Cream butter and sugar, add eggs, and then the flour (into which the baking powder has been sifted) and milk and flavoring. Divide in half and bake one-half of batter in two layers, saving the rest of the batter to mix with the following ingredients:

1 TABLESPOON MOLASSES   2 CUPS RAISINS

SOME NUTS OR CITRON

1 TEASPOON EACH OF CINNAMON, CLOVES AND NUTMEG

Bake two layers of this also, and put the dark and light layers together alternately with the following white icing.

ICING

Boil two cups of sugar in about two-thirds cup of water until stringy, and pour this gradually over the well-beaten whites of two eggs, beating constantly until thick enough to spread. Flavor as desired.

BLACK CHOCOLATE CAKE

¾ CUP OF SHAVED CHOCOLATE   YOLK OF 1 EGG

1 CUP MILK   BUTTER SIZE OF AN EGG

1 CUP SUGAR   1½ CUPS FLOUR (SCANT)

3 SCANT TEASPOONS BAKING POWDER

Put chocolate, the egg yolk and half of the milk in a saucepan and cook until thick, stirring constantly. When thick remove from stove, and add butter, sugar, the rest of the milk and flour, into which the baking powder has been sifted, and lastly the well-beaten egg white.

Bake in three layers, and put together with white icing above.

Be very careful not to get too much flour. It must be very soft and bake quickly.

GOVERNOR NORTHERN'S WHITE CAKE
(*used since 1880*)

8 EGG WHITES	2 CUPS SUGAR
1 CUP SWEET MILK	2 TABLESPOONS BAKING POWDER
1 CUP WHITE BUTTER	2 CUPS FLOUR
1 CUP CORNSTARCH	

Cream the butter and sugar, add the milk, then flour (into which the baking powder has been sifted) and the cornstarch. Add the whites, stiffly beaten, and bake in cake pans about one inch deep. Put together with white icing.

SPICE CAKE
(*From Gate City Cook Book*)

1 CUP SUGAR	1 CUP SOUR MILK
1 CUP MOLASSES	3 EGGS
1 CUP BUTTER	1 HEAPING CUP FLOUR
1 TEASPOON EACH OF MACE, CINNAMON, ALLSPICE, NUTMEG	
1/2 TEASPOON CLOVES	1 2/3 TEASPOONS SODA

Cream butter and sugar, and add egg yolks. Stir two-thirds teaspoon of soda into molasses, and add to sugar and egg mixture. Dissolve one teaspoon of soda in sour milk, and add this slowly, alternating with flour, then add spices, and lastly the egg whites. Bake in layer pans, and put together with white icing.

ORANGE CUP CAKES

Make batter as for the immortal one-two-three cake, using instead of milk, half water and half orange juice, then add the grated rind of one orange. Bake in individual molds, and ice with orange icing, or sprinkle with powdered sugar.

FRUIT CAKE

1 POUND BLANCHED ALMONDS	1 POUND DRIED FIGS
3 POUNDS RAISINS	1 POUND DATES
2 POUNDS CURRANTS	1 POUND CITRON
1 POUND CRYSTAL. CHERRIES	1 POUND CRYSTAL. PINEAPPLE

1 POUND ORANGE AND LEMON PEEL MIXED

1 ½ POUNDS LIGHT BROWN SUGAR

1 ½ POUNDS BUTTER	13 EGGS
1 ½ POUNDS FLOUR	1 TUMBLER BRANDY

2 TABLESPOONS EACH OF GROUND CINNAMON, MACE, CLOVES, ALLSPICE AND NUTMEG

1 TABLESPOON OF SODA IN A LITTLE WATER

Cream well sugar and egg-yolks, add a little flour and a bit of each fruit, a little at a time, until all fruits are mixed with the flour that is left after sifting over the fruits when they are cut into small bits. This keeps them from sticking together so badly. Add the spices and egg whites, then brandy (sometimes gin can be used with sherry wine) and lastly add the soda which has been mixed with lukewarm water.

Line a big pan with three layers of greased paper and bake for many hours. Any bakery shop will bake this better than can be done at home and at a reasonable rate.

JAM CAKE

3 CUPS FLOUR	⅔ CUP BUTTER
2 CUPS SUGAR	4 WHOLE EGGS
1 CUP JAM (ANY KIND)	1 CUP BUTTERMILK
1 CUP CHOPPED NUTS	1 TEASPOON SODA

1 TEASPOON EACH OF ALLSPICE, CLOVES, MACE, CINNAMON
AND NUTMEG

Cream butter and sugar, add yolks, a little flour, then jam, more flour, whites of eggs, nuts, spices, and lastly milk into which is dissolved the soda just as ready to use. Place in greased layer-cake pans and cook for twenty minutes in rather hot oven. White icing is better with this cake than any other, as it is rich enough without a heavy frosting.

OLD-FASHIONED BLACKBERRY ROLLS
(Other fruits may be used)

Wash berries carefully and put into round pan with sugar. Let this cook for a few minutes until very hot and sugar well dissolved. Make pastry. Take one heaping cup of flour, a pinch of salt, one teaspoon baking powder, and a heaping tablespoon Snowdrift. After sifting the flour, salt and powder together, and adding the shortening, stir in enough milk to make a very stiff batter. With a large spoon drop this into the pan of hot berries and juice. This will float on top. Bake until the crust is very nice and brown, sprinkle with a little sugar and serve in deep saucers. Hard sauce should be used on top of this dessert.

CARAMEL CAKE

One cup of butter, two cups of sugar, two and a half cups of flour, sifted twice, four eggs beaten together until light and foamy, one and one-half teaspoons of baking powder, vanilla. Bake in moderate oven in three round or two square pans.

FILLING

Three cups of granulated sugar, one cup of cream, one scant cup of butter; mix well, put on stove and boil until clear. While the above is boiling, melt one cup of sugar over a slow fire until dark brown. Add to the above, let it boil up well together, then remove from fire, and beat until thick and won't run off cake.

PLAIN LAYER CAKE

One and one-half cups of sugar, one-half cup of butter, three cups of flour, one cup of water, two eggs, two teaspoons of baking powder, one teaspoon of flavoring. Bake in shallow tins about twenty minutes.

ICING

Four ounces of chocolate, one-half cup of milk, one cup of sugar, one teaspoon of vanilla.

CINNAMON BREAD

1 CUP SUGAR	1 EGG	¼ CUP BUTTER
½ CUP MILK		1¾ CUPS FLOUR
1½ TEASPOONS CINNAMON		3 TABLESPOONS SUGAR
¼ TEASPOON SALT		3 TEASPOONS BAKING POWDER

Cream butter, and add sugar gradually, then egg, milk, and lastly flour sifted with baking powder and salt. Put in a greased pan about eight inches square. Mix cinnamon and three tablespoons of sugar and sprinkle over top of mixture, and bake about twenty minutes. Cut in squares and serve hot.

FAIRY GINGERBREAD

1 CUP BUTTER	1 CUP MILK	2 CUPS SUGAR
4 CUPS FLOUR		1 TEASPOON BAKING POWDER
	1 TABLESPOON GINGER	

Beat butter to a cream, and add sugar gradually. When very light add the ginger, then the milk, and, lastly, the flour in which the baking powder has been sifted. Spread very thin on bottom of upside down pie tin and bake.

COLONIAL COOKIES

Mix one cup of butter and two of sugar, add two well-beaten eggs, and one-half cup of milk, in which one teaspoon of soda has been dissolved. Stir in gradually one and one-half cups of flour, roll, cut in shapes and bake.

NUT BREAD

2½ CUPS SIFTED FLOUR	I CUP CHOPPED PECANS
½ CUP SUGAR	3 LEVEL TEASPOONS BAKING POWDER
½ TEASPOON SALT	I CUP MILK	I EGG

Mix dry ingredients, then add milk and eggs, well beaten. Bake one hour in slow oven.

SOFT GINGERBREAD

Put in a large bowl or pan, two cups of molasses (Sorghum syrup is the best) and two-thirds cup of shortening. Heat to boiling point, and add three full teaspoons of soda, and beat hard. Add two well-beaten eggs, and one cup of sour milk, then the following dry ingredients, previously mixed together—four cups flour, one tablespoon ginger, one tablespoon cinnamon and any other spices you wish, one teaspoon salt. Bake in moderate oven ten or fifteen minutes.

The batter should be rather thin in the pan, as it rises and is very light. This quantity will make a large biscuit pan full.

SOFT GINGER CAKE

One cup of sugar, one cup of molasses, one cup of butter, two and one-half cups of flour, three eggs, two and a half tablespoons of ginger, two tablespoons of cinnamon, one lemon—juice and rind—one-half nutmeg, one teaspoon of soda dissolved in one-half cup of hot water. Mix butter and sugar, rub together and add spices and lemon, eggs, then molasses, one-half cup of hot water with soda. Stir quickly and add sifted flour last. Bake in greased pan in moderate oven.

THIN GINGERBREAD

One-half pound of flour, one-quarter pound of butter, one-quarter pound of sugar, three eggs, one ounce of ginger. Mix well together, and roll as thin as possible on tin sheets, and bake quickly.

COOKIES

Two cups of flour, one cup of sugar, one-half cup of butter, one egg, two tablespoons of milk, heaping teaspoon of baking powder. Flavor with lemon. Make dough, roll and cut and bake in biscuit pan.

SWEET WAFERS

3 EGGS, BEATEN LIGHTLY   2 TABLESPOONS BUTTER
½ LARGE CUP SUGAR   1 CUP FLOUR
½ TEASPOON VANILLA

Mix into thin batter, and put teaspoonful in wafer iron at a time.

PAN CAKE

One pint of milk, one-half pound sifted flour, two eggs, one-quarter pound of butter. Beat eggs and add one gill of milk. Stir the flour with this until it becomes a very smooth paste, then add the rest of the milk. Stir in the butter, warmed to be soft, and if lumpy, strain. Put a small lump of butter in a pancake pan; when hot, pour in two tablespoons of the batter, spread it so as to cover the whole pan. Fry until a light brown on both sides. Roll the cakes and sprinkle with soft sugar. Serve hot, and eat with sherry wine.

"A GREAT CAKE"

And if you think these receipts are a little rich for the times—read about the cake which Martha Custis made for her grandmama at Mt. Vernon in the Year of our Lord 1781, and you will concede that we have taken a few steps in the right (?) direction since those days.

This was copied from an old manuscript dated Mt. Vernon, 1781, and is entitled

"HOW TO MAKE A GREAT CAKE"

"Take forty eggs and divide the whites from the yolks, and beat them to a froth.

"Then work four pounds of butter to a cream, and put the whites of the eggs to it, a tablespoonful at a time, until it is well worked.

"Then put four pounds of sugar, finely powdered, to it in the same manner.

"Then put in the yolks of eggs and five pounds of flour and five pounds of fruit.

"Two hours will bake it.

"Add to it one-half an ounce of mace, one nutmeg, one-half pint of wine and some French brandy.

"This was made by Martha Custis for her grandmama."

SOME OLD TELFAIR RECEIPTS

A series of old notebooks, preserved in the archives
of the Telfair Academy of Arts and Sciences, formerly
the home of the Telfair family, who left this house to
the City of Savannah for an art gallery, are filled with
many practical receipts written by Miss Mary Telfair [1]
in a fine and careful hand.

Sandwiched in between practical suggestions for the
care of slaves—such as economy in shoes, a cure for
hysterics, and for the ague and for dropsy—are lists of
parlor games and charades, of "nostrums for fashionable
entertainments," and some delectable receipts for angel
food, floating island, snowballs, and other old-fashioned
desserts—a few of which are appended here. [2]

GREEN GAGE PRESERVES (TELFAIR)

Take the gages when nearly ripe. Cut the stalks
about one-half inch from the fruit, and put them in
cold water with a lump of alum the size of a walnut. [3]
Set on slow fire and let simmer. Take them off fire and
put in cold water. Drain and pack close in preserving
pan. Pour over them enough clarified sugar to cover
them, and simmer two or three minutes. Set them by

---

[1] Miss Telfair was the Aunt of Ward McAllister, to whom the Earl of
Shaftesbury refers. See page xvi.

[2] These receipts have not been tested. They sound a little vague, but
quite intriguing, and the names are delectable enough to secure them
entrance anywhere.

[3] Every old kitchen must have been supplied with a walnut for meas-
uring purposes!

in earthen pan until next day. Then drain the gages and boil the syrup with more sugar until quite thick. Put on gages and simmer three minutes more, and repeat two days. Then boil clarified sugar to a blow. Place gages in glasses and pour syrup over, and when cold tie with a bladder and upon that a leather.

TRANSPARENT PUDDING (TELFAIR)

Beat eight eggs light. Put in boiler with one-half pound of sugar, one-half pound of butter, and some nutmeg and cook until thick. When cool, put a rich puff paste in dish, pour in the pudding and bake in a moderate oven. Add a little orange or citron.

FLOATING ISLAND (TELFAIR)

Mix three and one-half pints of milk with one-fourth pint of raisin wine, a little lemon juice and rose water and sugar. Put on top a froth made of white of egg beat up with currant jelly.

(This sounds more like a drink than a dessert, but not such a bad drink after all.)

SNOW BALLS (TELFAIR)

1 PINT MILK	1 POUND FLOUR	10 EGGS
6 OUNCES SUGAR	¼ POUND BUTTER	SPICES

Boil the milk, stir in the flour and butter, and when nearly cold put in eggs. Stir sugar in by degrees and fry in spoonfuls!

LEMON PUFFS (TELFAIR)

1¼ POUNDS SUGAR   GRATED RIND OF 2 LEMONS
BEATEN WHITES OF 3 EGGS

Beat an hour (!)—make any shape—cook on tin sheets.

ORANGE TART (TELFAIR)

Squeeze pulp and boil two oranges tender. Weigh and double of sugar. Beat to a paste, add the juice and pulp of fruit, and fresh butter the size of a walnut. Make puff crust and line pie tins. Put in mixture and make icing of yolk of eggs and melted butter. Mash flat with feather and sift sugar over it and put in oven.

PRESERVES AND PICKLES

THE FIG PICKER

THE OGEECHEE LIME

is a local variety of the Spanish lime—Melicoco Bijaga
—so called because they grow on the banks of the
Ogeechee river. They are very scarce in this country
and were probably left in this section by the Spaniards.
The negroes can always find a ready market for 'Gee-
chee limes during their short season, for they are considered a great delicacy, preserved, with meat and game.

OGEECHEE LIME PRESERVES

Cut off blossom end of limes and soak in alum solution (one tablespoon alum to two gallons water) for
twenty-four hours. Take out of the alum solution and

boil in clear water. Drain and put in a syrup made of one cup of sugar to one cup of water, a pound of sugar being allowed for one pound of fruit. Cook slowly until transparent.

PEAR CHIPS

Eight pounds of pears, sliced, seven pounds of sugar, four lemons, sliced, one crystallized ginger, chopped. Make a syrup of water and sugar, and boil fruit in it for two hours.

SCUPPERNONG JAM [1]

Pop the pulp out of the skins, says the very descriptive old receipt—and, in case you don't know just what that means, try squeezing a scuppernong and you will soon find out. Place skins in a vessel and cover with water, and let simmer until tender. Put pulps in another vessel and cook slowly until seeds separate, then put through colander to remove seeds. Put skins and pulp together, and allow three-quarters pound of sugar to one pound of fruit, and cook until thick. A most excellent accompaniment for meats, and a grand substitute for mince pie!

WATERMELON RIND PICKLE

Select watermelon with thick rind. Cut rind into small pieces and weigh. One melon usually makes

[1] A darker jam may be made with the Muscadine grape, or Southern Bullace.

about five pounds of rind, and this receipt is for that amount. Cut off all red and green from rind.

Make syrup of five pounds of sugar, two and one-half pints of vinegar, one ounce of root ginger, broken up, one-half ounce of cloves, one ounce stick of cinnamon, and let come to boil. Cover fruit with hot water and boil until you can pierce it with a straw. Then drain off the water and put fruit into syrup and let boil up once. Put in stone crock and let stay covered for three days. Then pour off syrup, and boil and pour over fruit in jars.

GROUND ARTICHOKE PICKLES

Put through a coarse grinder four quarts of artichokes and four large onions. Mix two and one-half cups of sugar, one teaspoon of tumeric, two tablespoons of celery seed, four tablespoons of salt, one-half teaspoon of red pepper with three pints vinegar. Add the artichokes and onions and let simmer thirty minutes.

ARTICHOKE PICKLES

I PECK ARTICHOKES	2 QUARTS ONIONS	2 CUPS SUGAR
I GALLON VINEGAR		I CUP SALT
I SCANT TABLESPOON TUMERIC		½ CUP MUSTARD

Put salt, sugar, mustard and tumeric in vinegar and let come to a boil. Wash and scrape artichokes and put in crock—a layer of artichokes, then a layer of sliced onions. Pour boiling vinegar over them.

JERSEY PEACHES

Pare one peck of large peaches. Put two quarts of water, two pounds of sugar, and one cup of vinegar in a kettle. Drop peaches in, and as soon as thoroughly heated, put in air-tight glass jars, and pour the syrup over them.

FIG CONSERVE

4 POUNDS FRESH FIGS, WASHED AND PEELED

2 LEMONS   I POUND SEEDED RAISINS

3 POUNDS SUGAR   I CUP PECANS

Cut figs and lemons fine, add sugar (no water) and cook until very thick. About one-half hour before done add raisins, and stir in the pecans after it has been taken from the fire.

SPICED FIGS

6 POUNDS FRESH FIGS (CELESTIALS)

3 POUNDS SUGAR   ½ OUNCE CLOVES

I OUNCE ALLSPICE   I OUNCE CINNAMON

I QUART RED VINEGAR

Soak figs for ten minutes in six quarts of water and one cup of soda. Wash in clear water. Put sugar, spice and one pint of vinegar to boil. Let boil hard, then add figs and boil twenty minutes. Take figs out and drain. Add the other pint of vinegar to the sugar and vinegar mixture, and let boil until thick. Pour over figs and seal while hot.

GRAPEFRUIT MARMALADE

One grapefruit, one lemon, two oranges, four pounds of sugar, two days.

Cut fruit with scissors into small pieces—skin and all. Soak in water twenty-four hours, then boil for one and one-half hours. Take off stove and add sugar and let stand another twenty-four hours. Then boil hard for one hour, or until thick.

This amount fills eight jelly glasses.

BITTER ORANGE MARMALADE

This is much more delicate and unusual than the average orange marmalade.

Cut twelve oranges in half—across the fruit. Remove pulp and cut up oranges very finely. To each pound of fruit add three pints of water, and allow it to stand twenty-four hours. Place pips (seed) in basin, cover with water and let this stand twenty-four hours also.

Strain off and add juice to fruit which has been standing. Boil this two hours or until tender. Then cool and add one and one-quarter pounds of sugar to each pound of fruit and juice. Boil about three-quarters of an hour after adding sugar, or until it jellies.

APPLE CHUTNEY

3 QUARTS APPLES—CUT UP   3 POUNDS GRANULATED SUGAR
1 POUND SEEDED RAISINS
1½ ORANGE SKINS, FINELY CHOPPED
½ PINT STRONG VINEGAR   ¾ PINT WATER
½ TEASPOON GROUND CLOVES

½ TEASPOON CINNAMON
1 CUP PECAN NUTS, CHOPPED FINE

Boil together until tender. This makes about three quarts of chutney, and will keep indefinitely in glass jars. Fine with chicken, mushrooms and game, and especially good with wild rice.

BRANDIED PEACHES

4 BASKETS PEACHES   3 POUNDS SUGAR   3 PINTS WATER

Pour boiling water over peaches, peel and throw into cold water. Make a syrup of the water and sugar, and when it comes to a hard boil throw in the peaches and let them cook until slightly tender. Take out and put in jars. Cook syrup until thick and pour over them, adding brandy if possible. The proportion is one quart of brandy to two quarts of syrup.

PEACH CONSERVE

4 POUNDS PEACHES   1 POUND SUGAR   1 GRATED LEMON
1 GRATED ORANGE, SKIN AND ALL
½ POUND ENGLISH WALNUTS

Peel peaches and boil until pulpy. Add sugar, lemon, and orange, and cook until thick. Then stir in chopped-up nuts, put in jars and seal. A delicious mixture for peach ice cream in winter. About one and one-half pints of conserve to one quart of cream makes a delectable desesrt.

PEACH PICKLE

Use Elberta peaches—not fully ripe. They are just as good as clingstones and far easier to eat. Peel fruit and stick three or four cloves in each one. To ten pounds of fruit use five pounds of sugar and one quart of vinegar. Cook together until a straw can be stuck in the fruit. Take peaches out and cook syrup until thick. Or heat syrup and pour over fruit for three consecutive days.

PEPPER RELISH

12 GREEN PEPPERS	12 RED PEPPERS	6 WHITE ONIONS
1½ CUPS SUGAR	1 PINT VINEGAR	SALT

Put peppers and onions through meat grinder (coarse cut), sprinkle with salt, pour boiling water over them, and let stand until cold. Drain water off and add vinegar and sugar. Boil twenty minutes.

CANDIES

BENNE CANDY

Benné is an East Indian herb—called Sesame in the Orient—which is supposed to be a charm with which to secure entrance and exit through any portal. It was this magic which Ali Baba employed to swing the doors of the treasure cave—his "Open Sesame!"

The slaves brought it to this country from Africa, and it is to be found today in many of the negroes' gardens. They make benné candy and benne cakes from the seed for sale in the market, and are said to pound the bean into a kind of paste which they eat on their hominy.

But, most interesting of all, is the fact that, although they never heard of Ali Baba and his magic words, they sprinkle it on their doorsteps to bring them luck and ward off ha'nts!

Boil together

1 POUND BROWN SUGAR	½ CUP MILK
SMALL LUMP OF BUTTER	1 TABLESPOON OF VINEGAR

When beginning to thread, take off stove and beat into it one and one-half cups of benné seed, which have been carefully picked, and parched. Add one teaspoon of vanilla and beat until creamy. Drop a teaspoon at a time on a buttered dish or paper and let cool.

CREOLE KISSES

Beat the whites of three eggs very stiff with one-half pound of pulverized sugar, one-half teaspoon of cream of tartar and one teaspoon of vanilla. Old receipts say beat one-half hour, but the electric beater does it in about twenty minutes, and gives you just enough time to be getting your pecans cut up, and your pans lined with brown paper and well greased.

When the egg mixture is stiff enough to "peak," beat in a cup of pecan meat, and drop a teaspoonful at a time on well-buttered brown paper, and bake in a very slow oven about one-half hour.

If the oven gets too warm, open the stove door, or turn off the gas until it cools off. The meringues should really *dry out,* not cook quickly. If you want them a golden brown, turn up the heat for a few minutes.

This amount makes about three dozen kisses.

PECAN SQUARES

Beat four eggs light with one pound of medium brown sugar. Cook this in double boiler for twenty minutes. Take off stove and add one and one-half cups of flour (in which one and one-half teaspoons of baking powder have been sifted), one teaspoon of vanilla, and one and one-half cups of chopped pecans. Spread half an inch thick in greased, floured pan, and cook twelve minutes. Cut into squares.

PECAN NUT CANDY

Boil together one can of Eagle brand condensed milk (no other), two cups of brown sugar, one lump of butter and one teaspoon of vanilla. When done, beat thoroughly and add one cup of pecans.

GRAPE FRUIT CANDY

Soak the peel of three grapefruit in water and salt overnight. Drain off next morning. Cover with cold water and cook about two hours, changing water three times. Take out of water and slice into small strips. Put one and one-half cups of sugar with one-half cup of cold water to boil. Put fruit in this and let boil slowly until all the syrup boils away. Roll in granulated sugar while warm, and let stand until cold.

NEW ORLEANS PRALINES

Put one cup of sugar in a saucepan with just enough water to cover well. Cook until it ropes slightly. Add about a teaspoon of butter, one teaspoon of vanilla and two cups of pecans, chopped. Stir hard until creamy, and drop or roll into balls.

CHOCOLATE CARAMELS

I CAKE BAKER'S CHOCOLATE	I CUP BROWN SUGAR
3 LIGHT CUPS GRANULATED SUGAR	I CUP MILK
I STICK BUTTER I TEASPOON VANILLA	PINCH SALT

Cook until thick and let cool somewhat before beating until smooth. Pour on buttered dish and cut in squares. Like velvet.

LET 'ER RAIN!

If crops are suffering from lack of rain, and you feel constrained to do your bit by your country, plan to make peach leather, and you will bring down rain on the just as well as the unjust. It is as good as a garden party or a county fair to ensure a downpour, since the sun is the essence of the contract for making

PEACH LEATHER

One peck of peaches peeled and mashed through colander. To each gallon of peach pulp, add three-quarters pound of sugar, and let come to boil. Remove from fire and spread on tin pie plates, and put in the sun to dry. Old receipts say it should stay in the sun three or four days, being brought in at night. When dry enough to peel away from the plate, it is done. Sprinkle the top with sugar, cut in strips and roll into wafer-like pieces, of any length preferred. It will keep indefinitely in tin.

WINES AND BEVERAGES

GONE ARE THE DAYS!

In the good old days, apparently beyond recall, we always entertained our distinguished visitors with a bowl of famous Chatham Artillery Punch, whose origin dates back to Colonial days. The Chatham Artillery is the oldest military organization in Georgia, and the punch seems to have been as much a part of their outfit as the cannons which still grace every parade, though the punch, alas, is but a potent memory.

Tradition has it that when President Monroe was in Savannah in 1819, on the occasion of the sailing of the first steamship across the Atlantic, he was entertained on a river trip and made the acquaintance of Chatham Artillery Punch, and many a later celebrity has tested his ability to imbibe against that suave and deceitful brew . . . the receipt for which is hereby appended.

CHATHAM ARTILLERY PUNCH

1½ GALLONS CATAWBA	1½ QUARTS RYE WHISKEY
½ GALLON ST. CROIX RUM	1½ GALLONS STRONG TEA
1 QUART GORDON GIN	2½ POUNDS BROWN SUGAR
1 QUART HENNESSY BRANDY	JUICE 1½ DOZEN ORANGES
½ PINT BENEDICTINE	JUICE 1½ DOZEN LEMONS

1 BOTTLE MARASCHINO CHERRIES

Make stock with above from thirty-six to forty-eight hours before time for using. Add one case of champagne when ready to serve.

BACARDI RUM PUNCH
(*A substitute for Chatham Artillery Punch*)

4½ DOZEN ORANGES (CUT IN DICE)   5 DOZEN LEMONS
3 QUART BOTTLES MARASCHINO CHERRIES
6 LARGE CANS SLICED PINEAPPLES (CUT IN DICE)
3 LARGE CANS GRATED PINEAPPLES
4 QUARTS TEA (GREEN TEA: USE 1 TEASPOON TO
1 CUP WATER)
1 DOZEN BOTTLES CANADA DRY GINGER ALE
1 DOZEN QUARTS BACARDI RUM (OR CHARRED CORN)

Make stock two days in advance. Allow about four to six bottles of Apollinaris water to each gallon of stock.

CHAMPAGNE PUNCH

Mix juice of six lemons and juice of six oranges with sugar enough to make a thick syrup. Add two bottles of Apollinaris, and let stand until sugar is dissolved. Add crushed ice, and, just before serving, three bottles of champagne and one of Sauterne. Enough for twenty-five people (in past days).

MINT JULEP

Put a teaspoon of sugar in a tall glass or silver goblet. Add just sufficient water to dissolve sugar.
Break off tender leaves of mint and add to the syrup.
Crush mint leaves vigorously with a small wooden pestle.

Allow a jigger and a half of rye whiskey to each glass, and stir well.

Fill glass full of finely crushed ice, and stir again.

Add more ice and agitate gently.

Put slices of apple and orange and pineapple around the sides of glass, and strawberries and cherries on top, and lastly, sprigs of slightly bruised mint.

Sprinkle a little sugar on top . . . and sip!

GRANDMA'S EGG NOG

For one glass or portion, use one egg, one tablespoon of sugar, one to three tablespoons of brandy, gin or rye, according to strength you desire, and one gill of cream.

For a party, use twenty-four eggs, three cups of sugar, one and one-half quarts of brandy, and one quart of cream.

Beat egg yolks until quite mellow, and add sugar as if making a cake. It is very necessary that the eggs and sugar are well mixed, and all sugar grains have disappeared. Then add the brandy, very slowly, as the brandy cooks the eggs if added too rapidly. When this has been finished, fold in the cream, well beaten, and the whites of the eggs which have been stiffly beaten.

AFTERNOON WINE PARTIES

In *Society as I Have Found It*, Ward McAllister gives the following account of afternoon wine parties in Savannah in the old days.

"You were asked," he says, "to come and taste Madeira at 5 P.M.[1] after your dinner! The mahogany table which reflected your face, was set with finger bowls, with four pipestem glasses in each bowl, olives, parched groundnuts and almonds, and half a dozen bottles of Madeira. There you sat, tasted, and commented on the wines for an hour or more."

Verily, there's nothing new under the sun!

Today we swap receipts, and try to imagine we are getting an effect with the various concoctions upon which we experiment. . . . Try this one, made from our native scuppernong grapes. It is about as near to a real Sauterne as you may find on a long summer's day.

SCUPPERNONG WINE

Wash and dump the grapes into a first-class, watertight cask, barrel or crock. Do not add any water or sugar, but merely mash the entire contents into a pulp— the more they are mashed, the better.

Allow the mash to remain exposed overnight, so that it will ferment, and give it another mashing next morning.

After the mash has fermented one day, or, perhaps two (not longer), squeeze it through a cheesecloth bag. To each gallon of juice add two and one-half pounds of granulated sugar.

Make sure that the sugar is thoroughly dissolved. Put the mixture in the cask, or crock, or receptacle

---

[1] The custom of dining between two and three o'clock is still observed in some Savannah homes.

prepared for it. Fill right up to the top, and allow it to bubble away for a couple of days.

After the fermentation has pretty well spent itself, skim, and place the cover (or bung if it is a cask) through which you have previously inserted a glass tube, carefully on receptacle, and seal it tight by the use of paraffin or wax. Place a rubber tube on end of glass tube, and let end of rubber tube rest in a jar of water.

Let wine stand in this way for at least six weeks, then siphon off into bottles.

One peck of scuppernongs makes one gallon of wine.[2]

GRAPE WINE

2 QUARTS GRAPE JUICE	2 QUARTS WATER
1½ POUNDS SUGAR	2 POUNDS SEEDED RAISINS
	1 YEAST CAKE

Chop raisins, dissolve yeast in one-half cup warm water and mix all ingredients. Let stand in crock, covered with cheesecloth, for ten days, stirring daily with wooden spoon. Strain, and put back in crock for four days, then siphon into bottles, corking *lightly*. After two or three days, cork tightly.

ORANGE WINE

| 1 GALLON ORANGE JUICE | 1 GALLON WATER, BOILED |
| | 1 POUND SUGAR |

[2] The Muscadine, or Southern Bullace, a rich purple grape, can also be used for this wine.

Mix orange juice, water and sugar, and each day for three successive days add another pound of sugar. Let stand twenty-one days. Strain and bottle.

BLACKBERRY WINE

as made by a descendant of Savannah's most famous connoisseur—if you will leave it in peace long enough— is as mellow as good old port.

Select ripe blackberries. Wash and measure. To one gallon of fruit put one gallon of water and let stand twenty-four hours uncovered to ferment. Strain. To one gallon of this liquid add three pounds of brown sugar (enough to "bear" an egg as the old books say) and strain again, and put in casks. Leave open a few days until fermentation begins, then bung tight.

And—this is the hardest part of all—Let stand six months then draw off and bottle.

CHERRY BOUNCE

1½ POUNDS BROWN SUGAR   4 QUARTS WILD CHERRIES

1 QUART RYE

If you can get these ingredients, put them together and seal up for two or three weeks, then strain off and bottle.

RUSSIAN ICED TEA

(as served at Russian Embassy)

4 HEAPING TEASPOONS ORANGE PEKOE TEA (NO OTHER KIND)

4 QUARTS BOILING WATER   3 ½ CUPS SUGAR

HANDFUL MINT LEAVES   JUICE 4 LEMONS

Pour boiling water over tea, and let steep three hours. Make a syrup of sugar and a little water, and let mint leaves steep in this a few minutes. Then strain and add to tea. Lastly, add the lemon juice. Serve with plenty of crushed ice, one sprig of mint and one slice of orange.

This will keep for days in a glass jar in the refrigerator.

AN OLD-FASHIONED PICNIC

(From the journal of George Wymberley Jones De Renne.)

"April 12, 1878—Went down the river to Daufuskie and Tybee, in a steamer (*The Centennial*) chartered by me at $50.00 for the day.

"We left the wharf, foot of Drayton Street, at 9.15 A. M., arrived at Daufuskie (Bloody Point) at 11.15. Visited that place. Mr. Stoddard, Mrs. Habersham and myself and my gardener going in a carriage with me to Melrose for the two hours, the rest remaining at Bloody Point. . . . At 2 P. M. we crossed to Tybee, lunching enroute on boned turkey, sandwiches, rolls, crab salad, chicken salad, orange sherbet, strawberries and strawberry ice cream, snowball pound cake, 6 bottles of champagne, 2 of sherry, 2 of whiskey, lots of ice. Five rocking chairs (bamboo) for the ladies, from my house, and napkins, plates, dishes, tumblers, wine glasses, knives, forks, spoons, saucers, etc.

"Returned to Savannah, reaching wharf at 6.45 P. M. The weather was perfect and nothing untoward happened."

"March 20, 1880—Leta had a luncheon party at Wormsloe. They went by rail relieved by carriages. (Gave the Steward of the *Wyoming* $5.00 for case of butter)

"At the luncheon, Josiah Murray and brother waited. Annie Nuthall, Mathilda and Katherine in the kitchen. Oyster on the shell, boned turkey truffled, sandwiches, crab salad, and orange sherbet, cakes, strawberries, oranges, apples, prunes, dried ginger, coffee, burnt almonds, chocolate caramels. Everything cold, but coffee. Wines, even sherry and champagne. Weather charming."

*   *   *   *

Half a century has rolled by, and although we do not do things in so grand a manner these days, many of the old traditions which are observed still give an atmosphere of leisure and grace to customs which have persisted in standing out against progress and its devastating hand.

Some of these old receipts may seem complicated when compared to modern makeshift dishes, but they have stood the test of time, and are still used in many Southern homes where good cooking is considered so important a part of good living.

INDEX

INDEX